THE ART OF VOICE

ALSO BY TONY HOAGLAND

Poetry

Priest Turned Therapist Treats Fear of God

Recent Changes in the Vernacular

Application for Release from the Dream

Unincorporated Persons in the Late Honda Dynasty

What Narcissism Means to Me

Donkey Gospel

Sweet Ruin

Prose

Twenty Poems That Could Save America

Real Sofistikashun

THE ART OF VOICE

Poetic Principles and Practice

TONY HOAGLAND
with KAY COSGROVE

W. W. NORTON & COMPANY
Independent Publishers Since 1923
NEW YORK | LONDON

Copyright © 2019 by the Estate of Tony Hoagland

All rights reserved
Printed in the United States of America
First Edition

For information about permission to reproduce selections from this book, write to
Permissions, W. W. Norton & Company, Inc., 500 Fifth Avenue, New York, NY 10110

For information about special discounts for bulk purchases, please contact
W. W. Norton Special Sales at specialsales@wwnorton.com or 800-233-4830

Manufacturing by LSC Communications, Harrisonburg
Book design by Lovedog Studio
Production manager: Anna Oler

ISBN 978-1-324-00268-0

W. W. Norton & Company, Inc., 500 Fifth Avenue, New York, N.Y. 10110
www.wwnorton.com

W. W. Norton & Company Ltd., 15 Carlisle Street, London W1D 3BS

1 2 3 4 5 6 7 8 9 0

This book is for students of poetry,
especially my students

CONTENTS

I

INTRODUCTION

The Living Speaker

ONE OF THE MOST DIFFICULT TO DEFINE ELEMENTS IN poetry is voice, the distinctive linguistic presentation of an individual speaker. In many poems voice is the mysterious atmosphere that makes it memorable, that holds it together and aloft like the womb around an embryo. Voice can be more primary than any story or idea the poem contains, and voice carries the cargo forward to delivery. When we hear a distinctive voice in a poem, our full attention is aroused and engaged, because we suspect that here, now, at last, we may learn how someone else does it—that is, how they live, breathe, think, feel, and talk.

This collection of short chapters emphasizes the ways in which a strong poetic voice is connective, binding the speaker and the reader into a conversation compelling enough to be called a relationship. A poem strong in the dimension of voice is an animate thing of shifting balances, tones, and temperature, by turns intimate, confiding, vulgar, distant, or cunning—but, above all, alive. In its vital connectivity, it is capable of including both the manifold world and the rich slipperiness of human nature. At the risk of sounding naively patriotic, such aliveness of voice seems like a special strength of American poetry in the last hundred years.

You could say that, whatever the "matter" of a poem is, it is carried along on the fluid tide of a voice. If a poem is to some degree about "story" or "theme," then the medium that delivers that information is the dimension of voice. Alternatively, we could say that voice embodies, not any set of particular facts, but the presence of a self, a personality or a sensibility. Maybe a complex poetic voice even communicates the history of how that sensibility developed.

In pre-1900s English poetry, the poetic voice tended to be rhetorically lofty, authoritative, wisdom-dispensing, and high-minded. Consider, for example, the passionate but didactic voice of a poem like Wordsworth's "The World Is Too Much with Us":

> The world is too much with us; late and soon,
> Getting and spending, we lay waste our powers;
> Little we see in Nature that is ours;
> We have given our hearts away, a sordid boon!

Wordsworth's poem is delivered by a strong speaker, but not a very intimate one by our standards. Contemporary poetry, and the poetry of twentieth-century America, shifted the footing of much poetry to the conversational and the highly mobile speech register of one ordinary person speaking confidentially to another. Here is the opening to Eleanor Lerman's poem "Ode to Joy":

> Four drinks after nine o'clock at the
> sports bar down by the river—the river
> that is commanded by Newtonian forces,

or so they say. They also say that
particles collide, but I've never seen
that happen. And then, of course,
there is the theory that giant lizards
are patrolling outer space in spiny ships,

. . . .

From just eight lines of Lerman's poem we can deduce a lot about its speaker. She is both educated and unpretentious, of a bemused and skeptical temperament; she is a person who is frank, even blunt, freely imaginative and a little profligate. As a reader, on some level you might ask yourself: Am I going to continue reading this poem? And if so, am I going to keep reading because of the *story*, or the *voice*? Probably the latter.

What do we want from a contemporary poetic voice? One good answer to that question is that we want to feel that we are encountering a speaker "in person," a speaker who presents a convincingly complex version of the world and of human nature. When we commence reading a poem, we are starting a relationship, and we want that relationship to be with an interesting, resourceful companion.

II

SHOWING THE MIND IN MOTION

A WRITER'S ABILITY TO PROJECT A VOICE ON THE PAGE is the product of many distinct verbal skills, acquired from myriad sources and practiced a great deal. Good writing is built on a kind of athletic virtuosity, the assemblage and combination of different muscular movements, like those of a good dancer. If you broke down any sport into its constituent parts, you would discover that hundreds of precise muscular movements are required to swing a 3-iron, or catch a ground ball, or clear a high jump. A good poem is likewise a performance that emerges from a set of precisely coordinated and much-rehearsed skills.

One way to make a convincing poetic voice is to display the mind in motion, or the mind changing direction as it speaks. We like to say "I changed my mind," but the human mind alters its direction so rapidly and constantly, we might as well say "My mind changed me." In a poem, this changing movement can be represented in many ways. It can be embodied through a kind of stuttering hesitation, or by a spontaneous uncensoredness, or as a deepening tangle of psychology. It can be performed as anxiety, or carefree light-headedness, or as overconfident swagger, or as steady, painstaking thoughtfulness.

When we can *see* a speaker changing his or her mind while actually in the middle of speech, it catches our interest. For example, here are some lines from a well-known poem by Frank O'Hara called "Poem":

> I was trotting along and suddenly
> it started raining and snowing
> and you said it was hailing
> but hailing hits you on the head
> hard so it was really snowing and
> raining and I was in such a hurry
> to meet you but the traffic
> was acting exactly like the sky
> and suddenly I see a headline
> LANA TURNER HAS COLLAPSED!

O'Hara's poem features a chatty, spontaneous speaker who is rambling along, narrating without premeditation. The poem's lack of punctuation and the extended, breathless run-on sentence represent the stream of consciousness of the speaker's speedy and unedited mind—the mind itself, you could say, is "trotting along."

What makes the voice of "Poem" so appealing and memorable is the way the speaker corrects himself and his companion; the mind tumbles forward, commenting on the traffic and the weather and his upcoming meeting. "It was raining, no, it was hailing, no, it was snowing, I was in such a hurry, and suddenly . . ."; it is the *voice* we are listening to, not the story, really. O'Hara famously said that a poem was something one wrote instead of making a phone call to a friend, and his poems are indeed as conversational and friendly as phone calls. In "Poem" the tone of the address is familiar and intimate and unedited—you could even say *careless*—and the result on the page is that the reader himself feels included in the warm immediacy of the speaker's life.

O'Hara's poem displays how one feature of "voice" poems is a love of *process*, not the neatened perfection of *product*. The goal of the poem is not to conceal uncertainty and to deliver an airtight argument, or proclamation, or insight, not to arrive at some truth, but rather to display the nature of the speaker's "real-time" sensibility, including its tendency toward indecisiveness and self-contradiction. In reading a voice poem like O'Hara's it might be said that you can feel the physical rhythm of the speaker's breath; the poem is breathing.

Here's another example of an American poetic speaker whose mind is "in process"; Gerald Stern's poem "Blue Skies, White Breasts, Green Trees" displays the speaker's perceptions changing and revising as he proceeds:

What I took to be a man in a white beard
turned out to be a woman in a silk babushka
weeping in the front seat of her car;
and what I took to be a seven-branched candelabrum
with the wax dripping over the edges
turned out to be a horse's skull
with its teeth sticking out of the sockets.
It was my brain fooling me,
sending me false images,

. . . .

for what I thought was a soggy newspaper
turned out to be the first Book of Concealment, written in
   English,
and what I thought was a grasshopper on the windshield
turned out to be the Faithful Shepherd chewing blood,
and what I thought was, finally, the real hand of God
turned out to be only a guy wire and a
pair of broken sunglasses.

Stern's poem—though quite surrealist at some moments—is a catalog of perceptions and revisions. In fact, the poem, in its recounting of a long sequence of misperceptions, amounts to a description of life. Rhythmically, this litany resembles a stand-up comedian's narrative of misfortunes and recoveries, "What I took to be . . . turned out to be . . ." and we continue listening to find out what is going to happen next, sensing that it will arrive at disaster or revelation.

Another structural detail to notice in "Blue Skies" is the progressively escalating stakes of the poem, as it lists "errors" in perception that the speaker has made. From mistaking a woman for "a man in a white beard," the speaker progresses to mistaking a pair of broken sunglasses for "the hand of God." The speaker is wandering through the junk of creation, but we come to understand that he is a persistent and honest seeker, and that earns our respect. This escalation in stakes could be said to be characteristic of serious poetry: a good poem intensifies, increases, and then resolves tension. However, the main thing to notice in "Blue Skies" is the recurrent self-revising of the speaker's mind, and our consequent interest in the sensibility of this poetic voice.

Both Stern's poem and O'Hara's are fast-paced, but the act of poetic self-revising can also happen at a slower, more measured velocity. In Genevieve Taggard's "The Geraniums" we can see the speaker working through a sort of puzzle—carefully, patiently adding observations and qualifications as she goes. She seems to be explaining and reasoning as much to herself as to us, her readers; her poem embodies a believable, attractive tentativeness:

Even if the geraniums are artificial
Just the same,
In the rear of the Italian café
Under the nimbus of electric light
They are red; no less red
For how they were made. Above
The mirror and the napkins
In the little white pots . . .
. . . In the semi-clean café
Where they have good
Lasagne. . . . The red is a wonderful joy
Really, and so are the people
Who like and ignore it. In this place
They also have good bread.

Taggard's poem, delivered in its methodical meditative voice, is probing into a question of aesthetics: how, it asks, can these red geraniums simultaneously be false and yet beautiful?

What a remarkable mystery it is, the speaker marvels, that the soul finds nourishment in the modern world. And let us consider the loveliness of the humble. "Even if," she says, "just the same," "they are red;" "really," she says, as if persuading herself. Not only are they red, decides our speaker toward the end of the poem, as we watch her thinking: the red is "wonderful." And then, even after arriving at her superlative judgment, she must add the rather matter-of-fact, qualifying observation that the people in the restaurant nonetheless continue to—and always will, she seems to imply—ignore the beauty right in front of them.

"The Geraniums" is a poem that could be graphed by its quiet escalations and de-escalations of evaluation; the cogs and levers of the speaker's meditation are visible in the small qualifying clauses of the poem, which give and take back and give again as they work their way through. The poem is a debate of checks and balances that artfully, delicately characterize the world on the evidence of this local setting. The red flowers are a wonderful joy, but the café is "semi-clean." And, Taggard's speaker seems to be figuring out, so is the whole world. Yet in this world, too, they have "good" (not great) bread. In "The Geraniums," we watch the speaker perceiving, thinking, "making up" her mind, and thinking some more, as the poem maintains a delicate balance of curiosity, qualification, irony, and affection. As O'Hara's poem makes a case for the liveliness of plunging forward at a pell-mell pace, Taggard's poem makes a case for the believable grace and insight that is derived from going slow.

In each of these poems, the humanity of the speaker's voice is created and revealed through the record of its transformations. In them we see reflected the instability of our own ongoingly changing selves, and our affection and respect are earned by the speaker's persistence.

For exercises corresponding to this chapter, please see page 119.

III

THE SOUND OF INTIMACY

The Poem's Connection
with Its Audience

A SUCCESSFUL POEM IS VOICED INTO A LIVING AND compelling presence. This convincing representation of a speaker may be created by force, or intellectual subtlety, or companionability, or even by eccentricity, but it must initiate a bond of trust that incites further listening. That presence in voice is not always "intimate" in a warm, "best friend" kind of way, but the reader must be impressed that the speaker is a complex, interesting individual who is intriguingly committed to what she is saying, and how she is saying it.

Such presence is only sometimes created by brevity. Many gurus on the craft of writing declare that a writer should "make every word count." Yet in poetry, often the charm of voice is more important than economy. After all, most of our daily interchanges don't convey information in an economical manner. When we say "What's up?" or "Looks like rain," our speech isn't really about conveying *information*, but about signaling to the listener that someone is present and accessible—open to conversation. They are gestures of presence. How about them Seahawks?

All day, every day, those "uhs" and "ers" and "likes" pepper and salt our spoken interchanges. These "inefficiencies" of speech serve a purpose in building tone and voice; they "warm" and humanize poetic speech; and they have their own prosodic contribution to make to poems. These interruptives, asides, idioms, rhetorical questions, declaratives, etc., float through our sentences like packing material, which in a sense they are—they pack and cushion and modulate the so-called "contents" of our communications. And this technically "inessential language" creates an atmosphere of connectedness, of relationality.

Consider, for example, this list of words and phrases we use in conversation—inessential in information, perhaps, but highly effective in establishing an environment of companionable warmth. To use these gestures in poetic writing is to make the poem more oral, you could say, than literary; more spoken than written. Such spoken colloquial additives are one key to a poetic voice that connects:

Here's the thing	anyway
well, you see	hang on a sec
say what you like	don't worry
if you say so	laugh if you like
I'm the kind of person who	sure enough
know what I mean?	in other words
why bother?	

The specific lexicon of such speech additives and asides may change from decade to decade or according to region, class, and generation, but our daily speech is crowded with them, and they are an important element in creating the atmosphere of much contemporary poetry.

We can see this kind of conversational, gestural communion-making in the opening of Mark Halliday's poem "Population":

> Isn't it nice that everyone has a grocery list
>
> . . . .
>
> we all have a grocery list on the refrigerator door;
> at any given time there are thirty million lists in America
> that say BREAD. Isn't it nice
> not to be alone in this. Sometimes
> you visit someone's house for the first time
> and you spot the list taped up on a kitchen cabinet
> and you think Yes, we're all in this together.
> TOILET PAPER. No getting around it.
> Nice to think of us all
> unwrapping the new rolls at once,
> forty thousand of us at any given moment.

"Isn't it nice. Yes, we're all in this together. No getting around it. Nice to think of us all . . ."—one may detect an underlying irony in the speaker's assertion of community, but these vocal gestures are effective enough to pull us deeper into the poem. This speaker may turn out to be a "confidence man" with a trick up his sleeve, but we are attracted by such familiar flavors of speech, the way that bees are attracted to the blue juice of a melting popsicle.

Notice, in the opening of Maurice Manning's poem "A Blasphemy," how few words contain significant information. Its phrases, many of them, are scant in meaning but rich in the creation of intimacy, designed to warm and to draw the reader into a receptive auditory state. To begin with, the poem is addressed to the reader: "You."

> You wouldn't have believed it, how
> the man, a little touched perhaps,
>
> set his hands together and prayed
> for happiness, yet not his own;
>
> he meant his people, by which he meant
> not people really, but trees and cows,
>
> the dirty horses, dogs, the fox
> who lived at the back of his place with her kits,
>
> and the very night who settled down
> to rock his place to sleep, . . .

The proponents of aesthetic economy may declare that "every word should count," but what about "You wouldn't have believed it" and "a little touched perhaps"? These asides and insertions have more to do with the connection between speaker and reader than the narrative.

If we separate out the "inessential" words from Manning's sentence, we get a more economical but less homey narrative:

The man prayed for happiness—
not his own but happiness for
trees and cows and dirty horses.

The story is still here, and even much of Manning's rhythmic storytelling cadence, but the listener is now excluded from the storytelling relationship and from the warm firelight of the storyteller's voice.

Poetic intimacy means *confiding*, but the speaker we find ourselves in relationship with is not always conventionally nice or friendly. Another contemporary poet who excels in the mode of the confidential voice is Lisa Lewis, whose poems are tough and unsentimental in their monologues of women's lives and hardship. Yet though her worldview is unromantic, Lewis's frank speaker can create a confidential atmosphere through just a few gestures. Here is how Lewis begins the poem "While I'm Walking":

Sometimes I like to tell people how they should live.
I think because I know a few secrets I have the answers
To everything, and that's not true. But sometimes the
     people
I speak to in my overbearing way listen, tilting
Their heads a little, implying that they're not ready yet
To take my talk at face value. . . .

The small speech gestures that create an air of casualness are here—"Sometimes I like to," "I think," "I know a few." But

Lewis's voice fosters intimacy in another way too: the quick revelation of plainspoken self-knowledge. In the declaration of the five-beat first line—with its acknowledgment of arrogance, error, and imperfection—we know we are in the presence of a truly interesting and brutally self-honest character. That bold frankness is followed by her confession of her "overbearing" manner, and an additional, almost comic description of the skeptical body language of persons subjected to her lectures on life. This is a wonderful way to start a poem, and, sneakily, the tableau also mirrors the relationship between poet and reader. Like the listeners in her anecdote, the reader-narrator encounter is itself a real-time contract-in-the-making, one in which the narrator asks trust of a dubious listener, then has to prove herself worthy of such trust. As we wade into this poem, we are deciding whether or not to stay and listen to this speaker with her "overbearing" way.

A little later in the same poem, the speaker tells an anecdote that is similarly revealing of her self-knowledge, and unapologetically honest about her own flawed character:

Once I saw a man get mad because two people asked him
The same question. The second didn't even know of the
    first;
Anyone would've called the man unfair, unreasonable,
He stormed at the person who approached him
That unfortunate second time, and it was nothing,
Where's the restroom? or Where could I find a telephone?
He was a clerk, and the second person, a shopper,
    suggested

He "change his attitude" . . .

. . . .

But though it ruined their day it improved mine, I could rest
Less alone in anger and wounded spirits. That was long ago,

. . . .

><

Lewis's plain linguistic style might be described as "prosaic," that is, verbose and unpoetic, yet it compels us because her speaker tells more truth than we usually get, and she does so with a bluntness that tests the conventions of decorum. Lewis is a narrative-discursive poet in style, not a poet of lyrical language, but there is a rhythmic, businesslike terseness in her storytelling and thinking that is riveting in its purposeful informality. Her speaker captivates us for the duration of whatever she wants to say. That's what a voice poet wants to do: hook us and then escort us deep into the interior of the poem, which is also the interior of the poet, which is also the interior of the world.

In a world where, socially, we often feel stranded on the surface of appearances, people go to poems for the fierce, uncensored candor they provide, the complex, unflattering, often ambivalent way they stare into the middle of things. In a world where, as one poet says, "people speak to each other mostly for profit," it is exhilarating to listen to a voice that is practicing disclosure without seeking advantage. That is intimate.

For exercises corresponding to this chapter, please see page 124.

IV

THE
WARMTH
OF
WORLDLINESS

The Material-Verbal Imagination

IT MAY NOT SEEM IMMEDIATELY RELEVANT TO A DIS-cussion of voice, but part of the relationship a poetic speaker makes with the reader is the world the poem presents; simply on a material level, a poem embodies worldliness in the nouns with which it is furnished—barking dogs and bank tellers with smeared lipstick and teenage boys with Taoist tattoos. Some American poets mention Italian Renaissance paintings in all their poems; others automatically include graffiti-tagged brick warehouses. These "data" are a kind of "vocabulary" of reality that the poem is offering to the reader—a particular version of the world—and they play an enormous role in determining the reader's decision whether or not to dwell inside the poem.

Because recognition is itself a kind of bonding, the reader wants to enter a world that she or he is conversant with, one that is to some extent shared. That doesn't mean we are not curious, however, and we can be interested in entering a world whose vividness and flavors are strange. Of course, familiar worlds can be surprising, too. When T. S. Eliot published his early poems, readers were startled by the urban realism of his details, the stale beer smells and poverty he described in London streets. They recognized the landscapes he described, and recognized them as dismal, but they also felt woken up and energized by the radical appearance of such "raw" details in a poem.

We could call this the material imagination of a poem, and the way in which poets furnish their "worlds" makes a claim about their speaker's worldliness that is essential to their credibility. One poet's poem will contain a bottle of Chateau Margaux '66 and a waiter named Paulo; another will feature cornfields and a pet goat named Sally. Such details sketch the parameters of the speaker's experience, knowledgeability, and interest. Cosmopolitan, gritty, rural, bucolic, gothic, suburban—the material imagination of a poem suggests the sensibility of a world. Here is the beginning of a poem by C. D. Wright, whose title also serves as its first line—"Everything Good Between Men and Women":

has been written in mud and butter
and barbecue sauce. The walls and
the floors used to be gorgeous.
The socks off-white and a near match.
The quince with fire blight
but we get two pints of jelly
in the end. . . .
. . . You with a fever blister
and myself with a sty. Eyes
have we and we are forever prey
to each other's teeth. The torrents

go over us. Thunder has not harmed
anyone we know. The river coursing
through us is dirty and deep. . . .

Wright's poem—her work is often situated in the rural
American South—is an aesthetic manifesto of earthy materi-
alism, one that includes poverty and the imperfections of the
flesh, one where the flow of life is "dirty and deep." Wright's
voice is plain but always pungent and typically has a tone of
gritty, unapologetic heroism, too, about the stubborn endurance of the human spirit under not always hospitable condi-
tions. The quince has blight, but nonetheless makes jelly, and a
man and a woman are just mortal folk: "You with a fever blister
/ and myself with a sty." This is a material world, where teeth
do damage and the socks don't match, but it takes a particular
kind of attentiveness, a particular kind of poet, to turn such
facts into an anthem.

As Zen practitioners might say, two people looking at the same
mountain are not *seeing* the same mountain, and so poetic "worldliness" can take an infinite number of versions: the sensibility of
an individual artist is as distinct as a fingerprint. C. D. Wright
could accurately be called a "dirty" poet, but there are many
styles of dirty. Here is the opening of "Spring Trances," a poem
by August Kleinzahler:

Two snails have found the inside of a Granny Goose
Hawaiian-style potato chips,

the clipper ship on its wrapper
headed out from the islands

on a wind-swept main.

Like Eliot and Wright, Kleinzahler is looking downward at the ground, but "Spring Trances" is animated by an entirely different tone. This speaker is observant and whimsical; and though the landscape is initiated with a piece of litter, an empty bag of potato chips, the poet's vision also includes the vitality of nature—happy snails!—and the vitality, too, of wonder and fantasy, in the way that the very particular image of the Hawaiian clipper ship is brought romantically alive. Here is a worldly sensibility related to, yet different from, Eliot's, marooned in discarded wrappers on a narrow London street. In Kleinzahler's sensibility, trash is made marvelous by the creative interventions of fantasy.

Things are important, crucially important to a poem, and every good poet is a "namer" and a great lover of nouns. As Frank O'Hara says in his poem "Today," "harmonicas, jujubes, aspirins! . . . They're strong as rocks."

At the same time, the "world" inside a poem is also a fantasia of *language*, of words chosen for their sound and flavor. The physical world of a poem is inextricable from the stylistically distinct way in which a writer selects her or his language—the physicality of word choice, sound, sentences, and imagery. In

Derek Walcott's lush descriptive narrations, the sensuous world is distinctively physical and specific, yet also delivered through the prosodic sensibility of a particular poet. The vistas that furnish "Omeros" are as aesthetically transformed and spacious as those in the tradition of great landscape paintings:

> The drizzling light blew across the savannah
> darkening the racehorses' hides; mist slowly erased
> the royal palms on the crests of the hills and the
>
> hills themselves. The brown patches the horses had grazed
> shone as wet as their hides. A skittish stallion
> jerked at his bridle, marble-eyed at the thunder
>
> muffling the hills, but the groom was drawing him in
> like a fisherman, wrapping the slack line under
> one fist, then with the other tightening the rein
>
> and narrowing the circle. The sky cracked asunder
> and a forked tree flashed, and suddenly that black rain
> which can lose an entire archipelago
>
> in broad daylight was pouring tin nails on the roof,
> hammering the balcony. . . .

Because of Walcott's highly cultivated formal skills in meter and sentence making, the world in his poem is unfurled in a stately cadence, lush but uncluttered. Walcott's description here has a leisurely, almost novelistic pace, like a panoramic camera that sweeps wide and across before zooming in. Image and metaphor are here in plenty, but—in contrast to Kleinzahler's colloquial manner, for example—they yield their prominence to the governance of Walcott's rhythmic, unfolding sentences: "The sky cracked asunder / and a forked tree flashed." Here, where the perspective is closer to omniscient than intimate, we might almost overlook the dimension of voice that is our topic—but Walcott's masterful voice permeates the scene as a kind of overarching sentience. Like the conductor of a symphony, pointing first to woodwinds, then to strings, the voice orchestrates the recognizably earthy world into a fulsome presence.

Every good poet has a developed, specialized expertise in how she packages and delivers the world to the page, and her way with physical detail is part of what makes her voice recognizable. The poet Diane Seuss has a particular love of the singular ingenious image, and has a seemingly bottomless inventory of them at her fingertips. Just listen to the cascading catalog of worldly data that begins her poem "Let's meet somewhere outside time and space," whose title is also the poem's first line:

> between the Song of Solomon and Isaiah where someone
>   pressed a trillium,
> in the ice cream freezer at the State Line Dairy where the
>   black cherry was and is no

more, in the coffee can full of blue marbles, under the
    jewelry box ballerina's skirts,
in her labial folds, between the skin and the nylon stocking
    of the window peeker,

in the butterfly display case, in a cell of an abandoned
    prison or bee hive, in the feed
trough of the cemetery horses, . . .

. . . where fake fingernail meets real, in the deserted
velvet factory and tuberculosis sanitarium, in the forest of
    forsaken hair tonics,

between the *m* and the *e* in the word *amen*, in the drawer
    where the hammer
used to be, . . .

Image is a large part of Seuss's talent, but a tuned-in reader
can observe her distinctive ways of handling image—serving
them up like the scoops of ice cream she refers to. Seuss's
capacious premise—"let's meet somewhere outside time and
space"—allows her to cherry-pick images from anywhere at all,
and we admire the variety and freedom of the speaker's invention. In many of her images we recognize a subtle wittiness,
and we get a passing intuition of the darkness and carnality of
the mind behind a detail like the "labial folds" of the toy bal-
lerina. We also get a sense of the poet's "ear" for cadence and
for certain consonants and vowels, and how they go together,

as in "Between the Song of Solomon and Isaiah where someone pressed a trillium." The image is an elaborate one, both clever and beautiful, and is held together, songlike, by all those "ssses" and "uns." A world is being built in front of us, and its images and sonic texture communicate humor, irony, and darkness that suggest the character of the speaker in a manner very related to voice. Distinct imaginations like Seuss's have defining consistencies to them; one example here would be the way in which the ingenious zoom-in on the space "between the m and the e in the word *amen*" echoes the earlier image of the pressed-together Bible chapters. Seuss's poem is a litany and a collage of the material world, full of wonders and ironies, beauty and ugliness, and when we read the poem, with its long-winded, cascading sentences and rich texture, we are carried along inside the speaker's voice. We know this speaker is a worldly person, and our recognition of that worldliness makes us trust her.

A decade or so ago the writer David Shields published a book about writing called *Reality Hunger*, whose title suggests the deep craving in the postmodern soul for something more tangible than electronic information. We have a great desire to be brought once again into contact with the physical, sensuous, objective world. When the material imagination is at work, a good poem can deliver an encounter with moments physically vivid enough to answer that craving.

The stuff of our daily lives and the meaning-freighted relationship between things themselves—this scuffed shoe and that umbrella, the abandoned house on Hickory Lane where the crazy man sleeps on cold nights—create an atmosphere that shapes the audience's reception of the poem. All of it mixes into a kind of habitat that consciousness requires in order to expand and concentrate. As much as any novelist, the poet, with her voice, has to build such a habitat.

For exercises corresponding to this chapter, please see page 130.

V

THE TRIBAL BOND OF THE VERNACULAR

"I AM SO BUSTED," SAID THE TV EVANGELIST WHEN IT was revealed that he had given his wife a brand-new Cadillac, and everybody listening liked him even more for his figure of speech. That's the tribal warmth of the vernacular at work. *He speaks our language*, they think of a politician or a movie star, and they can't help feeling more connected to him.

Slang, idiom, colloquial speech, jargon, vernacular: these are some of the various terms for "localized" language, speech used in ways known to local and native speakers—whether it is an expression used by the residents of one county in northern Maine or a noun that exists only in German, like the word *Backpfeifen-gesicht*, which means "a face that cries out for a fist in it." Nationalities, professions, different cluster-communities of social class and ethnicity—we all have our self-identifying vocabularies. Whether you are a steelworker or a stockbroker, you probably possess a vocabulary that gives you pleasure to use with another of your tribe. We use our vernaculars in the way that animals deploy various smells and glands: to tell others who we are and who we are with. Or, conversely, maybe we use it the way chameleons use color: to blend in.

That vernacular connectivity can happen in a moment, and its effect on a listener is often subliminal. "My ex-husband thought that beer was a major food group," says the comedian, and everyone laughs because of the ring of that classroom nutritionist's phrase, "major food group." Songwriters are familiar with the concept of the *hook*; so are journalists and poets. A good idiomatic phrase in a poem can enable it to lift off at a crucial stage, by striking the chord of tribal lingo at the same moment the poem is on its way to other, more serious business.

Many voice poets are temperamentally drawn to the flavors and uses of vernacular culture-speak. Their poems traffic with the current zeitgeists of language. For example, here's the start of "Poem, Or Beauty Hurts Mr. Vinal," by E. E. Cummings, who loves voices and the idioms of culture-speak:

> take it from me kiddo
> believe me
> my country, 'tis of
>
> you, land of the Cluett
> Shirt Boston Garter and Spearmint
> Girl With The Wrigley Eyes. . . .

Cummings's poem ultimately turns into a denunciation of commercialized America, but its opening lines deploy the kind of hooks that draw a reader closer, into a sense of relation—from the idiomatic phrase "take it from me" (meaning, *listen*) to the slangy informal address of "kiddo," to the quick, ironic echo of a patriotic song, and finally through the recitation of familiar commercial product names. All this happens at high velocity, and, taken by storm, the reader figures out she is meeting a playful, trickster speaker—someone fluent in Americanese, who is trying to entrance and recruit us as companions on the spontaneous adventure of the poem.

One could say that the American vernacular, with its power to disarm, is a kind of wrapping paper that can be used to dress almost any material. In Marie Howe's "Reading Ovid," the speaker repackages classical myth in such a way that any contemporary audience can understand its relevance, can be entertained and horrified by the oldest of stories. Skillful use of the vernacular has everything to do with the poem's success:

> The thing about those Greeks and Romans is that
>   at least mythologically,
>
> they could get mad. If the man broke your heart, if he
>   fucked your sister speechless
>
> then real true hell broke loose:
>   "You know that stew you just ate for dinner, honey? —
>
> It was your son."
>   That's Ovid for you.
>
> A guy who knows how to tell a story about people who
>   really don't believe in the Golden Rule.

Sometimes I fantasize saying to the man I married, "You know
    that hamburger you just

gobbled down with relish and mustard? It was
    your truck."

"The thing about those Greeks and Romans . . . they could
get mad," begins the poem, and the Latin writer Ovid, born in
43 BC, is suddenly just a guy, honey, whose characters "gobbled
down hamburgers," couldn't keep it in their pants, and suffered
the revenge of their wives. The bridge between past and present, myth and daily life, is constructed effortlessly through the
charm of a vernacular translation.

Brian Doyle's "What People Say When They Mean Something
Other Than What They Say" shows a keen diagnostic ear for
the mechanics of the American social vernacular, the way that
certain common phrases communicate without getting uncom-
fortably specific. His poem offers a catalog of common phrases
of polite deflection. It explicates out loud the speech codes that
we usually employ on a subliminal level. Interestingly, the end
result is the same; the speaker wins us over with his appeal to our
sophistication as fluent tribal speakers. The reader, also an initiate
in the lingo of Americanese, feels naturally bound to the speaker:

I have become a broken student of things people say
When they mean something other than what they say.
I have been dealing with some things meant pregnant.

God gives all sorts of gifts meant an autistic daughter.
Trying to get centered meant finding a halfway house.
A little time off meant walking to the police station to
Hand over the rifle he had spent the whole night with,
Staring at the barrel, a shoelace attached to the trigger.

In "Let Me Handle My Business, Damn," poet Morgan Parker leaps into motion with the quickness and momentum of Cummings's poem, and makes evident another characteristic of vernacular poetics: its orality. Vernacular takes its cadences and vocabulary from spoken grammar more than from the written. One way both Parker and Cummings enforce that dimension of their poems is through their use of run-on enjambment; the effect is that the voice spills through the line breaks in an unpunctuated stream that *sounds* spoken:

Took me awhile to learn the good words
make the rain on my window grown
and sexy now I'm in the tub holding down
that on-sale Bordeaux pretending
to be well-adjusted I am on that real
jazz shit sometimes I run the streets
sometimes they run me I'm the body
of the queen of my hood filled up
with bad wine bad drugs mu shu pork
sick beats what more can I say to you
I open my stylish legs I get my swagger back
. . . .

The vernacular speaker appeals to the cultural savvy of the reader, often in a tribal way. But in the generally liberal realm of poetry, vernacular isn't necessarily exclusive and proprietorial, intended for a listener from the exact same demographic. It also elicits the audience's ability to track swift changes of register: to notice that the same speaker can use both shorthand and longhand, so to speak, can juxtapose "I am on that real jazz shit" with "pretending to be well-adjusted," "sick beats" with "on-sale Bordeaux." As English is a composite of many different regions and economic classes, many different source-tongues and a globally enriched vocabulary, the vernacular poem is capable of helping us access our own multicultural fluency. Like listening to different genres of music, surfing inventive poems like Morgan's or Cummings's causes one's hearing to grow more adept. The more broadly we read, the more able we are to enjoy changing flavors as well as content, and thus to become more verbally ingenious ourselves.

There are myriad species and subsets of vernacular. The specialized vocabularies shared by soldiers, teenagers, soap-opera watchers, or nurses can potentially be a powerful conduit in the poetic transmission. One of its pleasures is performative, the part of us that mimics and parodies, as well as the part of us that wants to blend in and belong. Who knows what the vernacular original of the poem "Swing" sounds like, or what social group it is spoken by? It is written by a contemporary Chinese poet, Hsia Yü, and the translator, Steve Bradbury, has rendered the Mandarin original into a mishmash of American bohemian hipster jargons:

It was light before I hit the sack and so I slept till four
The whole day good as lost but I was feeling mellow as hell

The spring breeze tugging at my elbow all those footloose
  years
But here at the fag-end of our millennium I'm becoming
  quite the cavalier

Whenever chance reunites us we always vie to see
Who can be the first to waste some so-and-so
But to do it with you know a little style
Dance partners, drinking buddies, fuck-buddies, kindred
  souls
Hardly seems to matter when you're sitting around the
  table
And get that good-fellow feeling all men are brothers
Everybody's got a cellular phone

Bumped into a junior high school classmate yesterday
How's life I asked not bad he said
Nothing to write home about but I just got myself off so
You could say I'm feeling pretty chipper
So I asked whatever happened to that cunt you slummed
  around with
And he said we're still getting it on

By whatever acrobatic transposition the poem comes to us
from Mandarin to English, "Swing" illustrates the deep appeal
of tribal linguistic flavor—and perhaps the universality of lib-
ertarian verbal swagger. Almost no line lacks a colloquial, idiomatic phrase or word that is "off-label"—drawn from outside
middle-class register. As readers, to feel our fluency and com-

prehension of such a specialized argot makes us perky and proud of ourselves. It is like looking through the glass wall of an aquarium and seeing that these life forms of language are life itself.

When we come across vernacular, slang, catchwords, and colloquialisms in a poem, one effect is to put us at ease, to lighten the mood. *This poem is on my side*, we think, *I get this—not like those poems we had to read in school*. For an artist, that moment of relaxation is the doorway of opportunity. A poem is a little movie, cut and shaped from the footage of ordinary life. Its vibrant familiarities please and entertain us to draw us inside. Then, if the poem is good, its artful intensifications change our experience when we walk back out the door.

For exercises corresponding to this chapter, please see page 133.

VI

WHOSE VOICE IS IT?

A Writer's Voice Is Made from Other Writers' Voices

EACH WRITER GETS HER OR HIS IDEA OF LITERATURE from somewhere—and it is often from the oddest, seemingly random sources: a mother reading Dickens to her six-year-old, or a boy encountering James Baldwin in a high-school English class, or a young woman reading a poem by Dorianne Laux in a doctor's waiting room. Suddenly the background noise fades, the print on the page grows crisp and magnified, the intricate music of words and sentences, the miracle, it seems, of language used with eloquence streams and unfurls with an utter genius and clarity, and a rapture is born. Or, you could say, a kind of obsession.

Whatever that trigger text might be, our encounter with it *imprints* us like a gosling that hatches from an egg and looks up at the face of its mother and knows it is a goose. "I'm a goose!" it says, in a fit of ecstatic identification.

My novelist friend who, in his twenties, stumbled on the prose of Cormac McCarthy may never recover from the impact of that writer's baroque, biblical style, in which ragged men on horse-back ride through apocalyptic landscapes of prose "like men invested with a purpose whose origins were antecedent to them, like blood legatees of an order both imperative and remote." Others, who read Joan Didion or Frank O'Hara or Tang Dynasty Chinese poets, were also intaglioed, impressed, embossed with the music of a certain vocabulary and sensibility.

How odd, then, that we should fervently believe in the "originality" of our writing, when it is clear that the self in words (like the self in life) is comprised from the intermingled, overlapping crosscurrents of so many others.

The truth is, a writer's voice is made from other writers' voices. Pieced together, picked and chosen, stumbled into, uninformed: influence seems like an involuntary series of contagions that eventually turns into a sort of vessel, or transportation system. As we acquire a sense of taste, and perhaps a sense of vocation, our reading becomes more directed and targeted, but we are bent and shaped and destined to be changed by the genius of others. Compare it to the theory behind cannibalism, if you like. One eats the heart of the admired one and becomes them.

The remarkable news is that this pastiche of voices results in the incarnation of a new poet, a new hybrid distillation of voice, capable of telling the story of experience in new, valuable ways. Even great writers are cobbled together out of other writers; Hemingway famously stole from and then denounced the work of Sherwood Anderson. W. S. Merwin, we can see, after translating Jean Follain, suddenly began writing short poems of rural landscape and the gossip of history. Each strong new writer is a deep student of what she has read and an amalgam of preexisting sentences and styles that have never been combined like that before.

The idea that writerly originality appears from nowhere, or exists as something in isolation, a thing to be guarded and protected from influence, is lunacy. Anyone who doesn't school themselves by deep, wide, and idiosyncratic reading is choosing aesthetic poverty. Such aesthetic cloistering is like protecting your virginity in the belief that it will make you better at sex.

VII

VOICE AS SPEECH REGISTERS

High, Middle, and Low

A HANDFUL OF TERMS INEVITABLY ARISE WHEN DIS-cussing the role of word choice in the construction of poetic voice: diction, tone, pitch, and register. These terms are not identical in meaning, but for simplicity's sake we will use the term *speech register* to sketch out the basic concept of high, middle, and low speech.

The "register" of speech is most often described by metaphors of *altitude*; we say, high register, middle register, or low register. These are different ways of describing the degree of formality of a particular speaker or piece of writing. Such registers of speech are the finely tuned mechanism that tells the reader something about who is speaking or how they feel about the subject they are speaking of. Is the speaker sophisticated, educated, average, plain, or vulgar? Is the speech pretentious, condescending, cold, flattering, daring, utilitarian, incisive, angry, or neutral? A host of nuances and implications are attached to all word choices and word combinations.

To read poetry with an attention to voice is to quickly become more conscious of speech registers and their intricate powers of inflection, and to grow alert to the ways in which a speaker is relating to her reader and her subject matter. Every good voice poet is skilled at the modulation of register.

Speech register is, as they say, not rocket science. It isn't necessary to be a literary scholar or analytically trained to understand what we already intuitively know as native English speakers. The whole history of our listening lives has already sharpened our instincts about speech register and about how our word choices vary situationally. You speak differently to your four-year-old daughter than you do to the bank manager.

In English, and in American English especially, speech register is a particularly potent and versatile element of poetic voice, because English has an extraordinarily large lexicon, or vocabulary. We have a rich reservoir of synonyms, or alternative ways of saying the same thing. Thus our poems have a vast range of expressive possibilities to choose from. Our inflections, connotations, and nuances transform depending on what signifiers we use.

The three sentences below have essentially the same narrative content, but their tones are distinct from each other in ways we recognize as a matter of voice, or inflection.

We had lunch at the 4th Street Diner.   (Middle)
We took our midday repast at Chez Panisse.   (High)
We pigged out at Burger King.   (Low)

Both the proper nouns and the verbs of these sentences tell us much about the speakers and the way they intend to be heard.

Elizabeth Alexander's poem "Boston Year" opens in a middle register, a pitch that is direct, clear, plain, and highly effective for her retrospective narrative.

> My first week in Cambridge a car full of white boys
> tried to run me off the road, and spit through the window,
> open to ask directions. I was always asking directions
> and always driving: to an Armenian market
> in Watertown to buy figs and string cheese, apricots,
> dark spices and olives from barrels, tubes of paste
> with unreadable Arabic labels. I ate
> stuffed grape leaves and watched my lips swell in the
>   mirror.
> The floors of my apartment would never come clean.
> Whenever I saw other colored people
> in bookshops, or museums, or cafeterias, I'd gasp,
> smile shyly, but they'd disappear before I spoke.

The middle register of speech—the one Alexander employs here—is the level at which most of our daily conversation takes place, and so we hardly notice it stylistically—it is the most "natural," neutral, and functional register, the one we use to say we are going to the store or to ask a friend to open a window.

Alexander's speaker describes encounters of ugly racial affront and prejudice, but the middle style she chooses for her narration is neutral and undramatic. Why? This matter-of-factness of tone isn't accidental; for one thing, it communicates the levelheadedness of the speaker's character in the face of insult, and perhaps in some ways her subsequent lack of expectation of the world. Perhaps this flat factual narration evokes our sympathy on her behalf, because she is not expressing it. Or perhaps the speaker is withholding her sympathy for her own former self until later in the poem. For the moment she wants to narrate the facts as they are or were, showing neither self-pity nor outrage, but leaving the reader to draw his own conclusions. Such an objective middle speech register is strategic.

By contrast, consider the opening of Mary Ruefle's pastoral poem, "Diary of Action and Repose," which is pitched at a higher, more ornate language register:

> In some small substation of the universe
> the bullfrogs begin to puff out their mouths.
> The night-blooming jasmine is fertilized
> in the dark. I can smell it.
> And then someone unseen and a little ways off
> picks up his flute and asserts his identity
> in a very sweet way.

Here is speech conscious of itself as a poetic performance, and we intuit that the speaker is enjoying her own constructions of language. Such a poem becomes more about the way the speaker speaks than what she is saying. "In some small substation of the universe" turns out to be a frog pond or riverbank. The speaker's vocabulary is not just polysyllabic and precise, but elevated, formal, and ornate. One effect of this register is that the speaker is linguistically asserting her own originality of perspective—she sees the world from a lofty distance. On the one hand, our speaker acknowledges the relative unimportance of her personal landscape when compared to the universe itself; nonetheless, the bullfrogs are here and the night-blooming jasmine—and her elaborate language dignifies and ennobles them.

"Diary of Action and Repose" is about the beauty of an idyllic moment, and we sense that the poet is herself in a languorous mood, in no hurry to rush through her pastoral narrative. Her verbal constructions are ornate in a way that relishes its own expansions and contractions. Where this speaker could have said, "Someone is playing a flute," she says instead that someone "asserts his identity in a very sweet way." Like the earlier phrase about the substation of the universe, the thought encoded here is not just stylistically but also conceptually complex—to play music, the speaker implies, is to "assert your identity." The observation leads the mind of the reader into an interpretive digression. We enjoy the polysyllabic indirectness of Ruefle's constructions, and we know that we are in the hands of a confident and stylish speaker who is showing off a little, inviting us into the dance of language as much as into a story. This is a sophisticated lyricist.

In the middle of this performance, however, we encounter an abrupt appearance of plain, middle-register speech: "I can smell it," says the speaker. Such a sentence shows us the way in which different speech registers interact and counterpoint each other in the progression of a poem. It is like watching a dancer in the middle of a long flying leap put one shoe down firmly on the ground, as if to say, "I am ordinary, too, and I know where I am." *I can smell it.*

Another, quite different example of high-register speech can be found in the opening of Robert Pinsky's poem "Evolution of the Host," in which the speaker uses a detached scientific or anthropological diction to describe the evolution of human beings. The tone captures our attention with its stilted, "textbook" artifice, especially when we recognize that the poem is describing the very act in which the poem is engaged—the miraculous act of human speech:

> The primate that rose to dominate that planet
> Communicated with its peers in a code of grunts
> Exhaled from the orifice of ingestion and shaped
> By lips and inner membranes, muscles and teeth.
>
> The creature communicated with its descendants,
> By memorizing chains of those same brute sounds
> In patterns urgent as the dance of a worker bee
> Miming the distance and bearings of the pollen.

The tone of "Evolution of the Host" may seem strangely clinical, even frigid in its rhetorical distancing, but it renews the story from this uncommon approach. The effect serves one of poetry's many potential possibilities: to make something new and, in its way, freshly wondrous by defamiliarizing it. Here, the agent of the strangeness is diction, or speech register, pitched in the affectless vocabulary of a rigid university lecturer. Like the sample from Ruefle's poem, Pinsky's speech register is "high" and erudite; but where Ruefle's register is self-conscious, playful, and self-admiring, Pinsky's speaker articulates with an austere objectivity, dedicated solely to the information of his discourse. Here, an analytical vocal detachment is part of what makes the poem compelling.

High and low speech registers are more self-conscious in their pitch than the middle speech register. They call attention to themselves, and they often identify their speakers as sophisticated or vulgar, high-class or low-class in origin or intention. A high diction may be an attempt to impress the reader, and a low-class speaker might try to shock us—as the Latin poet Catullus often does. But to put it like that is not entirely accurate, either. It might be truer to say that voice poets are just talkers who love to try on different ways of saying a thing. Poets who love the exercise of voice are curious, unafraid, and enjoy themselves in the exhilarating game of exaggerated speech.

Catullus, famous for his erotic vulgarity, thoroughly enjoys the lower speech registers. In "This One Boy II," he insultingly addresses an erotic rival:

> Aurelius, king of gluttons once and future,
> you want to fuck my love, and you don't hide it.
> You're always there, flirting;
> you hang on him, try every line
> but all in vain: I'll snag you
> before you set the snare.
> If you weren't so skilled I'd shut up,

but now the boy has learned lust
and thirst—lay off, and I'll lay off;
if not, you'll find me up your ass.

Catullus wants to shock us a little with his graphic bluntness and violence of emotion, and he could be called the "most real" of the three poetic speakers featured in this chapter. Surely he is the least polite, the least elegant, the most passionately "visceral" in his reactions to the world. This voice combines anger and humor, and makes full acknowledgment of the carnal, beastly aspect of human nature. Paradoxically, however, the speaker is having a good time in his social warfare of love, lust, and insult. Even in less-skilled hands than his, the lower registers of speech—vitriol and profanity—have undeniable force; they radiate life, gusto, and heat, and that helps explain why Catullus's poetry—when not being culturally censored—has been popular for two thousand years.

Part of what draws us to poetry is a love of language and the myriad ways it can be twisted, augmented, and torqued. A voice poet is skillful at this kind of linguistic manipulation, often shifting registers in a way that surprises or delights or terrifies her reader. The more poems we read, the more we become comfortable with, and sensitive to, variations from the middle register of daily speech. Such deviations are exciting, be it an elevation or demotion from the normal level of diction, or an exaggeratedly idiosyncratic manner of speech. Much can happen on the page that doesn't or can't or won't in life. The voice poet invites the reader to join him in assuming a register regal and distant, like Ruefle's, or hot and close, like Catullus's. In poetry, the full range of human nature is on exhibit, and the performance on the page liberates us from our habitual self-restraint. Even when a poet stays steadily within a single speech register while reporting on heartbreak, as in Alexander's poem, that too can elicit complex recognitions in the reader. The speech registers of a poem not only reveal who their speakers are but also, in some way, provide readers with access to dimensions of their own selves.

For exercises corresponding to this chapter, please see page 138.

VIII

IMPORTED VOICES

Bringing Other Speakers into the Poem

FROM OUR PREVIOUS DISCUSSIONS, IT MAY BE GROW-ing clearer that a poetic speaker—or indeed, any human self—is not some pure, unified, and isolated entity, but a collection of linguistic gestures, influences, and impulses. Even one speaker is an assemblage, a collage of learned speech patterns, collected idioms, borrowed stances, and sometimes contradictory ideas, diction, and feelings. Our inner lives, as represented by the voices we carry inside us, are not fixed monologues, but a dancing and dialectical community of voices.

And if a poem is a kind of microcosm of how the world and the self continually intersect, how do we represent it? If, as poets, we wish not to oversimplify, or conceal, or sterilize the rich ecosystems of human linguistic consciousness, what should we include? That is the question we are repeatedly facing. Many different techniques exist to prevent us from such oversimplification. One method is the use of imported speech.

When a poet allows secondary speakers into her poem (even if she makes them up), it becomes less linear, more texturally diverse, and more dynamically driven by plot. Here, for example, is the opening of "A Manner of Speaking and Dying," a poem by the Brazilian poet Adélia Prado, translated by Ellen Doré Watson:

> He had a way of saying the word unshakeable.
> The final "l" sounded like the Dutch
> preaching to us: catechism, obligations, Sunday Mass.
> "Unshakeable certainty," "unshakeable faith," "power
>   unshakeable."
> When he used this potent word, he didn't say it
> with the mouth of someone who eats perishable substances
>
> . . . .

Simply by introducing another character, and his favorite word, "unshakeable," the narrator of Prado's poem is immediately provided with an adversary. The poem becomes an antagonistic dialogue between, not just two persons, but two types of speech and two ways of looking at life. In this case Prado's speaker is implicitly also in dialogue with her own past and the oppressive certainty of religious education. By opening with a sample of imported speech, Prado's poem swiftly engages in a forcefully represented struggle, one that is both intellectual and emotional.

Many of the best poets are skilled ventriloquists, which is to say they are mimics and samplers, adroit connoisseurs of different kinds of speech. In ways that are both obvious and subtle, they can incorporate a great variety of diction and linguistic registers into their poems. To import speech from outside the self and embed it in the text of a poem is a potent technique for rendering the social dimensions of voice.

If one thinks of a poem as a kind of ecosystem, to use imported speech is like introducing an additional species into the landscape—increasing its diversity and increasing the possibilities for conflict, wit, and contrast between the narrator's speech style and that of the visiting character.

Most important, perhaps, the use of imported speech pries the poem out of the managerial hands of the speaker and breaks the possible monotony of being overly anchored in the autobiographical mode. For indeed, poems that are too relentlessly contained in the voice of a single narrator can feel narrow and monotonous.

Using imported speech can also allow the speaker of a poem to introduce, or to smuggle in, different textures of speech, from the vulgar to the ornate. By embedding a contrasting type of speech against another voice, the poem's speaker gains the opportunity to exhibit rhetorical elegances and styles that might otherwise ring false.

In Stuart Dischell's poem "Lively in the Twilight with Abandoning Fleas," the speaker commences plainly and then raises the rhetoric by inserting an invented secondary voice, a more elevated poetic version of himself:

> Having observed a dead dog along the curb
> A person like me concludes,
> "Dead Dog, along the curb,
> Modest as you are, covered
> With a striped towel like a patron stretched out
> On the bench of the eternal sauna,

You are not an auger of ill,
But a recognition of the end
Of one thing and beginning of another."

"You are not an auger of ill," says the speaker—such baroque language might seem pretentious and melodramatic if presented directly in the poem's conventional contemporary voice, but because the high speech is situated against a highly realistic scene, and pronounced by a primary speaker who usually talks plainly, the poet can access the ornate beauty of a romantic and paradoxically dignified style.

For the reader, this juxtaposition is a source of both intrigue and pleasure, because we are granted the shapeliness of high language while, at the same time, allowed to retain a certain critical distance. Here is how the poem continues:

A person like me concludes,
"Dead dog, you are the ravished bride of the hour
Although I have not yet glimpsed your sex."
A person like me concludes,
"Dead dog, you are darkness's pup,
A weaned beast of life, forever absent at the teat,
Your footprints like black spots upon the tongue."

The speaker of Dischell's poem is well aware of the difference between elevated and ordinary speech, the high and the low. His technique of setting one apart from the other through quotation marks allows him to juxtapose them in a way that illuminates and validates the truth of each. These bursts of rhetorical and imaginative flourish are presented as self-consciously "poetic," yes; nonetheless, they add a heightened and signifying rhetoric to the poem, no less satisfying for their secondary status. A "dead dog" may remain the poem's undeniable, humbling occasion, but we understand from this alternate language that death itself is an authentically profound mystery, one that our narrator is aware of. We also are given to recognize that he is himself a person of various and interesting dimensions.

Marianne Moore often performs a similar game of combining high- and low-speech bytes. Some of her poems are composed almost entirely of disparate, pieced-together secondary sources. In her poem "Values in Use" Moore uses the importation technique to pronounce abstractions that might seem pretentious or overly bossy if spoken in the voice of the poem's primary speaker. By attributing the assertion to an outside source, Moore brandishes the starchy certainty of authority. Here are the first three couplets of Moore's poem:

> I attended school and I liked the place—
> grass and little locust-leaf shadows like lace.
>
> Writing was discussed. They said, "We create
> values in the process of living, daren't await
>
> their historic progress." Be abstract
> and you'll wish you'd been specific; it's a fact.

In this short passage, we first see Moore establish a baseline of plain-style speech—one who would say of her college, simply, "I liked the place." Then she imports a declarative professor-like voice that speaks in the imperious "we" pronoun. Then she adds a rather tart counter-commentary. By the end of these six short lines, we have a sense of the speaker's voice and character—distant yet offhand, discerning yet also colloquial: "It's a fact."

All these poems, we can observe, are fantasias of conversation—between characters, real and imagined, pushing and pulling at each other through different kinds of dialogue or dialectic.

As Dischell's poem shows, one doesn't necessarily have to introduce a secondary character into a poem to employ the technique of counterpointing speech styles. A writer can use her or his own speech as a kind of "quoted" vernacular that serves to launch a drama of contrasting styles or points of view. For example, in his poem "So I Said I Am Ezra," A. R. Ammons's speaker initially assumes the rhetorically commanding voice of a biblical figure, and then fluidly places that speech style into a kind of conversation with the unsubservient forces of nature:

> So I said I am Ezra
> and the wind whipped my throat
> gaming for the sounds of my voice
>   I listened to the wind
> go over my head and up into the night
> Turning to the sea I said
>   I am Ezra

but there were no echoes from the waves
The words were swallowed up
  in the voice of the surf
or leaping over the swells
lost themselves oceanward
  Over the bleached and broken fields

. . . .

There is a kind of oratorical grandeur to the dialogue Ammons creates, but also a pleasing loose-jointedness that arises from the conversational structure of the narrative. Ammons's speaker may have the big first word ("I"), but the landscape he is encountering is clearly answering, and deflating the egotistical pretension of the speaker with its indifferent natural forces.

In fact, we "quote" ourselves all the time in life, whether we are talking to ourselves internally, planning a future conversation, or replaying a remembered encounter with the world. "I told her, 'Are you crazy? There is no way I am going to loan you rent money again.' " "I told him I was going to take it up with the committee, and terminate his ass." We are the hosts of many kinds of talk. Why not get them into the poem?

Terrance Hayes's poem "All the Way Live" throws several kinds of imported speech into its short narrative about a dangerous, comic youthful prank:

"Do all dudes have one big testicle and one little tiny one?"
Hieronymus asked, hiking up his poodle skirt as we staggered
Down Main Street in our getup of wigs and pink bonnets
The night we sprayed NEGROPHOBIA all over the
  statue of Robert

E. Lee guarding the county courthouse, a symbol of the
  bondage
We had spent all of our All-the-Way Lives trying to subvert.
Hieronymus's thighs shimmered like the wings of a teenage
Cockroach beneath his skirt as a bullhorn of sheriff verbs
Like *Stop! Freeze!* and *Fire!* outlined us. . . .

Hayes's narrator has his own rich vocabulary in the poem, but
his lines are peopled and salted with "sheriff verbs" like *Freeze*
and *Fire*, and by his companion, with the unlikely name Hieronymus, anxiously asking about his testicles while they spray the
sociological term *Negrophobia* on the Robert E. Lee monument
in a Southern town. By using imported speech as one ingredi-
ent in the narrative, the poet skillfully creates the equivalent of
a multiple-car crash between adolescence, comedy, gender, the
history of American slavery, and law enforcement—a kind of
collision that, come to think of it, has a long, profoundly mixed-
up legacy behind it.

To write of the world, and into the world, means to become a
listener, and to hear the energy of other persons' language in different contexts and registers becomes a rich resource. Alone, or
together, we continue to observe, we are so complex.

One can hear the reward for such attention in the polytonal texture of a poem like "For Emily (Dickinson)" by New York School
poet Maureen Owen, which pastes together a variety of voices and
stories of the kind we encounter in the social world—"For Emily
(Dickinson)" uses poetry as a kind of environment portrait:

The girl   working the xerox in the stationary store
has a "thing"   for one of the customers   "I'm in love!"
she blurts to complete strangers buying stamp pad ink.
"Am I shaking?   Last week when he came in   I
stapled my thumb."   It's not just a shift in season
but a hormone that sets the trees off too   from plain
green they go   cheeks flushed   & dropping
everything!
Like the baby bashing through them   hooting   "More!"
&   the radio   announcing   "It's a Sealy Posturepedic morning!"
the landscape's gone silly   with abundance of motif. . . .

Owen's poem cuts and pastes together commercial language, the manic chatter of a crushed-out salesgirl, observations of seasonal nature, baby speech, and the literary analytic diction of "abundance of motif." The result is a whirling cinema verité that marries speech manners and the details of the world.

When attuned to the outer world in this way, we come to realize that the *self* is also internally diverse, both social and isolate, pragmatic and wistful, detached and compassionate. Our very thoughts, our most casual and most formal, petty and heavy remarks, are in a constant colloquy or conversation.

Owen's poem is a celebration of the milieu, of the manyness of any moment—it demonstrates how the use of secondary speakers in a poem often provides an amplification of poetic possibility; it will push the poem into unexpected currents of narrative, or repartee outside the reach of the wisest monologue. It issues an

invitation from the writer to his or her own deep imagination—
to start a fight, or start remembering something that never happened. Many people think of a poem as a one-person vehicle, like
a car with only one seat in it. But as soon as your dead grand-
mother starts talking, or a teenage barista with a nose ring asks,
"What can I get you?" another kind of dreaming begins. The
use of secondary speech has no limits as a poetic tool; not only
does it enlarge the poem into a social forum, it opens endless
structural possibilities.

For exercises corresponding to this chapter, please see page 144.

IX

VOICES BORROWED FROM THE ENVIRONMENT

NOT ALL VOICES ARE BROADCAST FROM A "SELF," AN individual human being. Not all poetic voices gain their flavor from the source of personality, a singular identity responding to experience.

Poets also borrow and paste and ventriloquize voice styles from the public zones of language—commercial, scientific, bureaucratic. These other forms of rhetoric have as much utility in the making of poetry as the nervous high-speed monologues of Frank O'Hara, the humane vulgarity of Charles Bukowski, or the high-styled, ornate, dramatically intense voice of Sylvia Plath. What is more, because we are the common possessors of modern and American culture, we are deeply familiar with many of these "public-domain" voices; we understand them from experience; we know the context of their usages, and the connotations of their appearance in poems and speech.

In her poem "In Answer to Your Query" the poet Naomi Lazard ventriloquizes the tone and linguistic register of a corporate message:

We are sorry to inform you
the item you ordered
is no longer being produced.
It has not gone out of style
nor have people lost interest in it.
In fact, it has become
one of our most desired products.
Its popularity is still growing.
Orders for it come in
at an ever increasing rate.
However, a top-level decision
has caused this product
to be discontinued forever.

Instead of the item you ordered
we are sending you something else.
It is not the same thing,
nor is it a reasonable facsimile.

Lazard's poem performs a social comedy that replicates the experience of consumer depersonalization and the frustration of dealing with a corporate entity. As the corporate "message" grows more and more absurd, we are amused. But the greater lesson to be gained here, from a poet's point of view, is the hypnotic power of such a voice to a reader or listener. Our intense sensation of familiarity, born of endless and repetitive exposure to such formulaic language, draws us to this voice; impersonal as it is, we are part of its constituency. Even knowing better than to listen to such voices, they possess a power over us; the declarative syntax, the fictitious "we," the lingo of authority—"top-level decision," "sorry to inform you"—appeal to us. Lazard's satire is about the absurdity of modern life, yes, but we might consider also how, by stealing, counterfeiting, and subverting such public forms, we can harness them to more nuanced poetic agendas and usages.

Consider Adam Zagajewski's poem "To. . . ," addressed to the chairman of the board, Death, a monologue that we might call the polite appeal of a citizen to our corporate sponsor:

> Madam Death, I am writing to request
> that you kindly take into consideration
> an extension of my liability to
> the institution headed by you
> for so many centuries. You, Madam,
> are a master, a violent sport,
> a delicate ax, the pope, velvet lips,
> scissors. I don't flatter you. I beg.
> I don't demand. In my defense I have
> only silence, dew on the grass, a nightingale
> among the branches. You forgive it,
> its long tenure in the leaves of one aspen
> after another, drops of eternity, grams
> of amazement, and the sleepy complaints of the poor poets
> whose passports you didn't renew.

Though it employs much the same diction and speech register— the bureaucratic—Zagajewski's poem is poignant in a way different from the comedy of Lazard's poem. Why? Because the status of power is reversed in the latter poem. Here, the speaker is humble, powerless, and mortal, like all of us, subject to the whim of the "corporation" or "government" of fate. The speaker is vulnerable, and the poem's central metaphor has the precision of effectively framing our mortal situation in a cogent way—we are indeed like the minor employees of a vast, powerful, and unknowable boss.

When the speaker says, "writing to request / that you take into consideration / an extension of my liability to / the institution headed by you," he is a person requesting an extension on his mortgage, or rent: life. (A similar trope informs George Herbert's great poem "Redemption," in which the speaker addresses his Christian god as a landlord, asking for an improved earthly property.)

Our environments—social, commercial, public, transactional, entertaining—are rife with "voices" and linguistic resources like these, and they are available for conversion to psychological and artistic purposes. We can call such voices foreign and impersonal, invasive and manipulative—they are often all of those things— but they are not entirely foreign in one sense, for indeed, they are already inside us. Moreover, we are already deeply fluent in their idiom, their rhythms and cadences. We ourselves are chambers filled with such voices, and, awake or asleep, we hear them in our dreams. Just as they have cultural power, they have artistic potential.

Moreover, to "play" with them, and to subvert them, means that we take them into the power of our imaginative authority— we can use them to make the very beauty and meaning that they constantly attempt to steal from us.

Here's another example of such stealing and "repurposing" of a familiar public speech act from Mark Halliday's poem "Campaign Promise":

Under my Administration
(in which each Cabinet member will have many, many
    long legal pads)

if you were standing frozen in sweated confusion
at the Personal Furnishings rack
in a giant department store five days before Christmas
wearing a woolly jacket that belonged to someone long gone
and trying not to seem dangerous
under silver and scarlet decorations with no conception
of adequate reply to tremendous departures

you'd be a notable American event.

Halliday steals the authority of a preexisting, highly familiar piece of rhetoric: the promises made by every political candidate for office. "Under my Administration," they say, but Halliday subverts the formula to frame a tender personal moment. This seemingly simple yet skillful borrowing converts a rhetoric of empty promises and hot air into an occasion for affectionate witness. His speaker "sees" the "you" in her woolly jacket trying to make a decision about what to buy in a department store and describes the scene with compassion and a little humor. Dead language has been turned into living language, rhetorical manipulation into an expression of tribute and kindness.

Culture is a vast hive of discourses available for similar redemptions. In this category of "environmental" voices we could include many familiar ceremonial formulas of speech: prayers, curses, blessings, For Sale ads, cooking recipes, and wedding invitations. Such conventional formulas are not all baldly "impersonal," like the rhetorical officialese used in the preceding examples of poetic "repurposing," but neither are they typical poetic self-oriented expressions of individual personality.

For another example, consider the possibilities of recasting the contemporary genre of the wine review and the esoteric language of wine appreciation in a poem titled "Joe's Dad's Burgundy":

This proletariat vintage
which excludes nobody
should be drunk from an old beige coffee cup
with a chip in its lip

after a day of hard work
inside the huge cold auto plant
of stacking rubber tires
into long haul cargo-trailers.

By the second glass you will feel
that muscle in your lower back
which has been tightening all day
mysteriously loosen

as if someone turning
a large wrench
had reversed direction

and then you are home
and suddenly able to remember
the steady marriage of your parents,
and their immigrant parents, and theirs.

Laundry flapping on its lines
above the neighborhood
that has not been gentrified

and your Polish nana
still walking around upstairs
getting supper ready for the family
thirty years ago,
in her orthopedic shoes.

You go online and order a case of it.

"Joe's Dad's Burgundy" shows, like other models in this
chapter, that our poetic notion of our own utter "originality"
is a myth. Indeed, we are the possessors of many different cultural forms and jargons, many registers of language and idiom
and discourse. In the making of art and meaning we are free to
invoke and harness their stylistic manners as much as our own.
That is the truth—when we enter poetic language, we are tak-

ing possession of the larger world, exploring its residual implications, redesigning and perhaps even improving its purposes. In this way, a poem can be seen as a natural form of political engagement, a supremely adaptable cultural instrument capable of much more than sounding off about a particular speaker's inner life.

For exercises corresponding to this chapter, please see page 149.

X

"SAY IT. SAY IT."

The Voice of Authority

WHAT IS THE MYSTERIOUS ORIGIN OF THE AUTHORITY found in the voices of some poems? Where does a writer get it from? When Muriel Rukeyser says, in this excerpt from her poem "The Speed of Darkness," "Say it. Say it. / The universe is made of stories, / not of atoms," we are moved, excited, and intimidated by the brave authority of her assertion. Declaration is one of the things that attracts us to poetry, and it is also one of the things that makes poems forceful, memorable, and useful.

It is frequently said that authority is *earned*—by age, for example, or through the painful endurance of hardship—but in poetry it is equally true to say that authority is *learned*, or even that it is *stolen*. We acquire the power to speak in an authoritative way by borrowing, memorizing, studying, and copying the authoritative speech gestures of poems we love.

Like all aspects of poetic voice, the source of authority in poetry is intricate and mysterious and takes many different forms. However, some of the skills involved in the production of an authoritative poetic voice are identifiable—and of these, one is the poet's ability to skillfully employ abstractions.

It may sound simplistic, or obvious, to say that part of the power of free-verse poems comes from the interactive dynamic between statement and story. But to study particular poems through this template can teach us much about how a strong poem is built. The relationship between these two elements of a poem—between abstract statement and physical detail—makes a fundamental claim on our attention as readers. After all, it mirrors the way we move through our lives: studying experience and attempting to derive general principles from it. The skillful orchestration of statement and image creates much of a poem's vocal authority.

The setting for Linda Gregg's poem "Fragments" is an underground subway car, late at night in the city. The speaker observes the pathos and unglamorous fatigue of the other riders. We've been here before, we readers, in life as well as in literature. Yet the abstract assertion in line five, when we encounter it, gathers the entire scene into a unified magnetic field:

> You can't call the exhausted people on
> the 1 or 9 line beautiful. Especially
> the drunk at the back yelling and stumbling
> and grabbing the pole gracefully just
> in time. Beauty has a strangeness.
> The old man leaning against the cement
> column at the station on 42nd (when I
> changed to the N or R) has three holes
> in his pants. Neon and magazine covers
> about a new couple. I believe everyone
> is going home. This is the way.

"Beauty has a strangeness," says the speaker, a statement that switches on its intellectual light, so to speak, and gathers the whole poem into a singular frame. The reader must now reconsider all its details within this transfiguring context, within the "plot" of that generalized assertion.

Indeed, the poem's worldly descriptions now are changed, because they are filtered through the idea of beauty. We see that "Fragments" is making the case for a particular kind of beauty: the beauty of so-called ordinary reality, even in its most awkward, tawdry manifestations. Even in fatigue, asserts the poem, even in this flawed impoverished setting, beauty makes its appearances. Beauty cannot be stopped.

It is important to note that Gregg's abstraction is an intriguing and unexpected one, as opposed to a cliché like "Love is wonderful" or "Isn't life sad." Its singularity provokes the reader to reflect before consenting or disagreeing: *Does beauty have a strangeness?* The fact is, some abstractions are more interesting than others.

It is also significant to observe that the abstract assertion of "Fragments" does not narrow or "corner" the meaning of the poem. In fact, in a good poem, the details of the narrative develop and inflect the proposition of the poem, and vice versa. Between the two elements, idea and story, an interplay exists, which, if it succeeds, unites the poem into a satisfying dramatic whole.

When assertion and story work together, two kinds of pleasure are joined: on the one hand, the immediacy of a particular account of experience and, on the other, the more spacious, comprehending perspective of an intellectual—or, one could say, spiritual—overview.

Gregg's plain-styled poem is not a great work of art, but one feels the firmness of its structure and the clarity of mind that made it. "Fragments" is a performance of poetic authority, and its effectiveness arises from the ability to make a provocative assertion, and the placement of that assertion in relation to the rest of the poem.

What about placement? In Gregg's poem, the dominant assertion is placed near the center of the poem. But the governing assertion of a poem can be stationed at the very beginning of a poem, or at the end, or almost anywhere else along the way. The placement of statement has consequences for the poem and will create a different dramatic and aesthetic effect.

Emily Dickinson's nineteenth-century poem "Remorse is Memory awake," spoken with that poet's characteristic analytic precision, opens with a large, typically Dickinsonian assertion:

Remorse – is Memory – awake –
Her Parties all astir –
A Presence of Departed Acts –
At window – and at Door –

Dickinson, of course, has a talent for abstract declarations; in fact, her air of absolute certainty can sometimes make her an overwhelming poet to read. What makes her work rewarding, however, is the concision and originality of her assertions regarding the world. In this case of "Remorse," we are thrilled by the odd compactness of her insight: remorse *is* memory awake. Delivered in the poem's first line, Dickinson's compressed abstraction has something of the effect of an exploding bomb: in the first moment of encounter, the reader's mind is blown and must grapple to encompass the implications of the poet's idea.

Placement of the poem's main idea in the position of the first line takes great intellectual confidence, because it requires that the idea subsequently be developed in surprising ways; without further embellishment and complication, the poem would already be over. Fortunately, Dickinson doesn't merely let her thesis lie but pushes her subject into characteristically strange figurative directions. The succeeding lines of "Remorse is Memory awake" add color and particularity, image and metaphor to the abstraction—we find that to dwell in remorse means to live in a kind of haunted house, one eerily alive with the ghosts of conscience, at window and at door. Remorse is an affliction of the insomniac, awake in the middle of the night in a struggle with the past. Austerely delivered, the details are nonetheless poignant. Still, much of the force of the voice in "Remorse is Memory awake" stems from the placement of the poet's declaration in the first line.

In his rich narrative poem "ICU" Spencer Reece takes almost the opposite strategy from Dickinson. Reece places his most powerful assertion four lines from the poem's end, only after we are deeply immersed in his stories of working in the intensive-care wing of a Connecticut hospital:

Those mornings I traveled north on I-91,
passing below the basalt cliff of East Rock
where elms discussed their genealogies.
I was a chaplain at Hartford Hospital,
took the Myers-Briggs with Sister Margaret,
learned I was an *I* drawn to *E*s.
In small group I said, "I do not like it,
the way young black men die in the ER,
shot, unrecognized, their gurneys stripped,
their belongings catalogued and unclaimed."
In the neonatal ICU, newborns breathed,
blue, spider-delicate in nests of tubes.
A Sunday of themselves, their tissue purpled,
their eyelids the film on old water in a well,
their faces resigned in plastic attics,
their skin mottled mildewed wallpaper.
It is correct to love even at the wrong time.
On rounds, the newborns eyed me, each one
like Orpheus in his dark hallway, saying:
I knew I would find you, I knew I would lose you.

"It is correct to love even at the wrong time" says Reece's speaker, and this paradoxical truth, arriving in the context of the poignant narrative details we have already absorbed, has a resonance inseparable from its timing and placement.

Some postmodern readers and critics have asserted that a poet should not be didactic, should not presume to generalize about human experience—it is, they claim, arrogant and politically suspect. We are right to be suspicious of politicians and demagogues who practice a kind of bullying rhetoric, but many of us read poetry in order to *learn* as well as to be entertained. We enjoy being in the company of someone who knows what she is talking about, or who acts like she does. For the time it takes to read a poem, we will entrust ourselves, even subordinate ourselves, to a convincing speaker, and we will relish or be enraptured by their mastery. When you are in the hands of an assured language user and an experienced thinker or feeler—to surrender is one of the true pleasures of community and art.

For exercises corresponding to this chapter, please see page 152.

XI

CONCLUSION

The Multiplicity of the World and the Heroic Integration of the Self

"CONTRA-DICTION," WE COULD SAY, IS THE NATURE OF the world and of human nature as well. It says different things simultaneously and speaks in multiple registers. Maybe you are in a cancer clinic waiting room while a TV cooking show host explains to the haggard patients how to make the most delicious barbecued chicken. California, you read, has legalized marijuana, but you have just learned that your partner is having an affair. Or maybe you are sitting in a restaurant looking at a menu while the newscaster on the screen over the bar is playing footage of drone strikes in Syria. It's easy enough to ironize such postmodern moments, but we stand in the crosswinds of them every day, and they sometimes threaten to pull us apart. What can a poem do?

Well, a skilled poetic voice can personalize and frame moments in such a way as to grant them human meaning. A good poem can shape experience into a kind of tango that makes facts dance and shape-shift until we find we must reconsider once again; we must concede one more time that we are vulnerable to wonder, grief, outrage, and reflection. "Be afraid," said the French poet

Apollinaire: "Be afraid of the day you can look on a locomotive without a sense of wonder!"

The best word for this kind of poem is "dialectical" because it implies that the poem has no predetermined position in relation to experience. This poem does not merely present the speaker's engagement with a meditative problem, it displays the speaker's entanglement in experience. It shows the illusory nature of the problem as well as its fatal, perhaps immutable substance. The freedom of the speaker is to dance with circumstances, trivial and profound. The liberal gift of the poem is to show the reader that such a dance is possible, that in fact we are attempting the dance every day. Experience is many great conversations happening at once. A good poem orchestrates such conversations in a way that makes graceful theater of them. The trashy and the precious, the shallows and the heights of human nature, the ugly and the beautiful—inside the poem they coexist.

We would like to think that many of the poems in this improvised anthology exhibit, in their vitality, all the resources and virtuosities of poetic voice. The dialectical nature of the world is admired in the chapter on Worldliness; the fluent nature of the self is promoted in the chapter on the Sound of Intimacy; the cultural composition of the self is described in the chapters on Speech Register and Voices from the Environment; and the social hybridity of the so-called individual self becomes clear when we talk about the use of "Imported Voices" in a poem.

Implicit, fundamental, and paramount to our claims about the dialectical turbulence of experience and poetic voice is the idea that the speaker of a poem, in the end, *holds it together*. What we see in the unfolding of the poem is a heroic struggle not to be blown away or destroyed in the boiling contradictions of time and phenomena. The self may indeed be an uneasy coalition of impulses, influences, misinformation, and truth, but it is stubborn to survive and, in the end, it is loyal to its body, its identity, and its desire to dance another dance.

The poem enacts the challenges of the self, its precarious cohesion, its flirtation with disintegration, and its scramble to hold the pieces together in the face of not just adversity but also multiplicity. This dance or combat takes place on many levels of the poem, in more ways than any craft handbook could identify, but the dimension emphasized here is obviously voice.

No statement more concisely formulates this version of poetry than a sentence from Czselaw Milosz's poem *"Ars Poetica?"*:

The purpose of poetry is to remind us
how difficult it is to remain just one person.

Cohesion is difficult, Milosz emphasizes, but it is possible. Thus poems of experience bear the scars and wounds and scorch marks, even the imperfections that damage leaves on the soul, but a good poem also testifies to the triumph of still being able to speak. Poets are wounded like all other human beings, but they have somehow not been wounded into the condition of speechlessness. Not quite.

Here are a few poems that demonstrate, in the athleticism and adroitness of their voices, how, as the African American spiritual goes, the self wades through the muddy world and the soul got over.

Meredith Cole's "Relationships" is a narrative poem that combines an ample number of the skills discussed in the preceding chapters. It is confiding, social and worldly, and set in a world enriched by imported, juxtaposed voices. The resourceful and observant speaker is resilient in her negotiations between the internal and the external, the objective and the vulnerably subjective:

Let's have a long boring talk about our relationship
he said on the local that sped through the foreign town
toward a world famous hot spring. I was thinking
he said about Buddha and how I've obsessed
over his teachings but now I realize
Buddha was wrong to leave his wife and kids
to travel to foreign lands.
The local we rode was identical in fact
to trains destroyed by atomic weapons in the second
world war. The rings
knocked together overhead. I wanted to get drunk
in the rain with red flowers falling over me.
I wanted to be as the poets say
enflamed. Tiny parking lots rushed past
red flowers blooming here and there.
In each flower, the rain.
In each cup of water existed the future
[. . .] and its devastating consequences.

Though Cole allows the boyfriend-speaker in the poem to open and even to initially dominate the discourse, in fact the poem's narrator maintains control throughout. We can hear the speaker's editorial hand in the sly inflection of "long boring talk about our relationship." The boyfriend's reported speech is mundane, and the speaker's view of the boyfriend, we intuit, is rather cool and ironic. By midpoint, the speaker has shifted into an internal monologue, and the poem moves from an ironic mode to a progressively more lush, elevated, even ecstatic register. The language of poetry, she acknowledges, is what she truly wants, in vibrant, defiant contrast to the mundane domestic conversation that another part of herself is involved in.

> I wanted to get drunk
> in the rain with red flowers falling over me.
> I wanted to be as the poets say
> enflamed. Tiny parking lots rushed past
> red flowers blooming here and there.
> In each flower, the rain.
> In each cup of water existed the future
> conversation and its devastating consequences.

Notice that Cole has given voice to at least three distinct speakers in her poem: the primary narrator, the self-absorbed boyfriend, and the voice of the "poets." The resulting "conversation" presents a lucid panorama of familiar human conflicts. It shows how many different layers and zones of the self can coexist. Nor is the outer world excluded from the realm of

Cole's poem—note the presence of past wars represented by the Japanese train, not to mention the Buddha's poor domestic track record of "leaving his wife and kids." Boyfriend, Buddha, nature, history, poetry, and self are all talking to one another in the poem, whose title, "Relationships," becomes more resonant as our comprehension deepens. Registers of speech shift swiftly from the mundane self-absorption of the boyfriend to the "enflamed" longing of the speaker for beauty, even at the price of misfortune. Cole's poem crisply reveals a richly diverse sample of human experience. What do we really want from a poem? We want to encounter a version of the world and of human nature that is not overly simplified. Cole's poem provides that pleasure through its acrobatic dexterity with plot and the medium of voice. The conclusion of the poem spins into the kind of transcendental bewilderment we experience in extreme circumstances—a state of mind oddly close to the state of rapture.

The speaker of Kenneth Patchen's poem "The Orange Bears" is an adult recalling his childhood, set against the historical background of the coal-mining industry, in the era of workers' unions, in Wheeling, West Virginia. It is a narrative of innocence and natural beauty destroyed:

> The orange bears with soft friendly eyes
> Who played with me when I was ten,
> Christ, before I left home they'd had
> Their paws smashed in the rolls, their backs
> Seared by hot slag, their soft trusting

Bellies kicked in, their tongues ripped
Out, and I went down through the woods
To the smelly crick with Whitman
In the Haldeman-Julius edition,
And I just sat there worrying my thumbnail
Into the cover—What did he know about
Orange bears with their coats all stunk up with soft coal
And the National Guard coming over
From Wheeling to stand in front of the millgates
With drawn bayonets jeering at the strikers?

I remember you could put daisies
On the windowsill at night and in
The morning they'd be so covered with soot
You couldn't tell what they were anymore.

A hell of a fat chance my orange bears had!

"The Orange Bears" may be spoken by an adult in reminiscence, but it is very far from nostalgic; it quickly and sympathetically enters the speech register of the remembered child-self, as a kind of outraged plaintiff for the defense of that lost innocence: "Christ, before I'd left home." Like a legal brief, the evidence is brought forth in one long sentence of indictments, in which the child's imaginary friends, "the orange bears," are the proxy stand-ins for the speaker's unprotected former self, stranded in a world of pillaged nature, polluted air, and adult economic violence. Perhaps the most surprising defendant in this resurrected drama is Walt Whitman, whose idealistic book of poetry—*Leaves of Grass*, we can assume—did not keep its promise to the child speaker, who would take it "down . . . to the smelly crick to read."

As with the poem by Meredith Cole, one admires the number of diverse players who swiftly populate Patchen's poem: the orange bears, the poem's speaker, the speaker's child-self, the coal miners, and the National Guardsmen coming over to break the coal strike. Many layers of the world are arrayed and orchestrated with swift clarity. And then there is the book, "in the Haldeman-Julius edition." Notice how literature has a presence in the poem, even if an ineffectual one—Whitman, with his utopian promises, seems to be no help under these circumstances.

It is a fact that poems sometimes actually provide us with a tutorial in how to feel and how to think, not just by telling our stories for us or by publicly emoting over what is usually left private, but by actually guiding us through the step-by-step process of how to metabolize memory. Patchen's poem gathers its evidence and argument, then escalates emotionally to the outraged, outwardly directed exclamation of the last line. "The Orange Bears" manages to be both a political poem and a psychological one. In this case, one could even say they serve the same function—for to organize and focus the incoherent feelings of the individual self, which is subject to large, unexplained forces, is to legitimize them and provide them with an avenue for action.

It is the age-old artistic function of catharsis that Patchen's poem performs, and in the act of reading, the reader vicariously enters into sympathy for her own violated child's spirit. In that sense, this poem is one written in defense of the child.

Yet to say that Patchen's poem is mainly an enterprise of sympathy would be to ignore its sophistication. The poem also represents the voice of the self coming into adulthood, an adulthood more realistic, more powerful, stronger, and surer of itself.

So many of the skill sets of voice discussed in these chapters are evident in Patchen's poem, from the vernacular of "hell of a fat chance" to the fluent touches of speech register, "the Haldeman-Julius edition," that remind us we are also being guided by a mature speaker, one who can use a word like "jeering" as well as "stunk up." "The Orange Bears" is a dialectically masterful poem.

Adrian Blevins's poem "The X Games" offers one more example of the inclusive intelligence of the voice poem: polytonal, forceful in attitude, alternately rude and vulnerable, restless in spirit and keen in observation of the cultural and personal worlds.

In the poem's narrative, the speaker's young skateboarder son has come to tell her about another teenage skateboarder's serious accident. The speaker uses the occasion to contemplate her son and the arduous history of his conception and upbringing:

When Benjamin comes in and stands in the doorway

with his hands in his pockets, I think: *He's eleven years old and unquestionably maladjusted.* I say: *You're so beautiful,*

you should be in Hollywood and kiss him, kiss him,

kiss him. Ben is in fact quite good looking, despite
the six or seven thrasher boys screaming and stomping

inside his blood, wearing neck charms that look like dog
   collars.
Yet isn't it really just *Ben* standing there? He of the two

who without any papers snuck inside me during the 1980's

when all I wanted was out of my marriage or retarded
or departed? That's how angry I was, I don't mind saying:

that's how bad the sex was. For now Ben would just like
   to say

that Someone Someone broke his neck trying a backwards
   double flip
on his bike. I've seen it before: the boys coming out all hot
   and excessive

like they were born in Wheeling, West Virginia on a bank-
   rupt carnival

ride. When I tell Ben I'm writing this poem and need to
   know
the name of the boy who died on his bike, he just looks at me
   slow

and skateboards grinning down to Greenland Street.

I just stand there then, and let him go.

One might say that the poem creates a kind of split-screen vision; on one half of the screen, we are presented with the factual scene of mother and son in her study, her memory of his inconvenient birth, and the innately hazardous recreational activities of young men. On the other half of the screen is the ongoing, multiple-toned commentary of the speaker's interior reflections. We are first initiated into this complex double consciousness when we hear the son described in two contrasting ways:

I think: *He's eleven years old*
and unquestionably maladjusted. I say: *You're so beautiful,*

you should be in Hollywood and kiss him, kiss him,
kiss him. . . .

Two simultaneous perspectives, both believably valid, are expressed in highly different dictions, one couched in the psychological jargon of a sociological report—"unquestionably maladjusted"—the other as a purely emotive maternal overflow of affection—"You're so beautiful, you should be in Hollywood." Yes, this may be a portrait of a mother-and-son moment, but the speaker's adroit linguistic skepticism makes it clear that this mother is hardly blinded to reality by her own sentimental attachment.

Such a moment elegantly displays a central poetic skill: how a speaker can be both attached and detached at the same time, both subjectively loving and ruthlessly objective. The economy with which Blevins performs this maneuver sets the template for the energetic back-and-forth between narrative and internal commentary that will follow throughout the poem.

Is Blevins's a confessional poem? No. The abundance of theatrical exuberance on display implies that the speaker has substantial distance and freedom from her own narratives. No matter how drastic or pathetic the discourse might be, we, the readers, can sense that the author is having a lot of fun and is inviting us to join in the hijinks of the human comedy.

Within the first two sentences of "The X Games" another skillful touch is to be found in the repetition of "and kiss him, kiss him, kiss him." Again, this effusive verbal act brings into the poem a distinct poetic skill set—one in which language becomes physical gesture; for this chant, in its pulsing repetition, is an enactment. If anything, this rich invention heightens the counterpoint at work, between what we could call the "clinical mom" and the "mammal mom." Both moms, we are left in no doubt, are real.

In the next few lines, Blevins's speaker makes a move back into the reflective, detached half of consciousness: the measured coolness of "Ben is in fact quite good looking," followed by her unsentimental assessment of the mania inside this eleven-year-old skateboarding boy, a boy with a whole posse of miscreants "screaming and stomping / inside his blood."

The poem's next frame is an internal review on the part of the speaker of her own personal history, how Ben is one of two children who

without any papers snuck inside me during the 1980's

when all I wanted was out of my marriage or retarded
or departed? . . .

Again, the verbal resources here are considerable and various—vernacular, idiomatic, metaphorical, and grammatical. Though voice poems and poets can sometimes exhibit more verbal fireworks than substance, Blevins's verbal display is not merely for its own sake but is one that maps the manifold simultaneity of an individual consciousness, both sophisticated and primitive, adroit and clumsy. When the speaker asserts, for example, that the children "snuck" inside her "without any papers," she implies firstly that she was parasitically invaded, taken advantage of by biology. But she also invokes the rich metaphor of illegal immigration—which may seem even more prescient to us now in 2018 than when the poem was written.

Another grammatical ingenuity of this sentence is in the "unmatched" sequence of noun-objects: "all I wanted was *out of my marriage* or *retarded* or *departed*." The sequence introduces a flurry of connotations, suggestions that are not logically coordinated nor entirely grammatical. The meaning of the sentence, however, is utterly clear in the context of the speaker's psychology and narrative.

Without much confusion, of course, we can infer that Blevins's speaker probably means "When all I wanted was [to get] out of my marriage or [to be] retarded or [to be] departed." On the surface, it may be a verbal mangle, but for reasons of voice, the monologist has spontaneously compressed the conventions of lexical precision to a basis of rhyming sonic invention— (*retarded, departed*)—a kind of riff in which the rationale of word choice shifts. Jokingly, the speaker implies that she wishes she *had* been retarded instead of married (and implies that perhaps she *was* retarded enough at the time to make such a decision). In addition, one has to love the double entendre of the word choice "departed," which can and does mean both "to leave" and "to be dead," as in "dearly departed." Because the voice poet is operating on all levels of vernacular, speed, idiosyncrasy, and slang, we, the readers, are *listening* differently than we might be to, say, a poem by Seamus Heaney, whose work is more invested in story and imagery than rich vocal play. And we are deriving distinctly different kinds of pleasure as a result.

"The X Games" resolves in the way it began: on a solid narrative footing in which the son, Ben, skates away without saying anything further. The narrative of mother and son will go on, mysterious and damaged and affectionate and precarious. In the meantime, the relationship has been momentarily framed and mounted in all its complexity, animated by the multifaceted skill sets of American voice, deeply rooted in real life and marvelously articulate of the vulnerable cunning inherent in human nature.

The role of voice in poetry is to deliver the paradoxical facts of life with warmth and élan, humor, intelligence, and wildness. Such art requires a particular spirit and a particular set of skills that the preceding discussions and examples try to exemplify. In the end, perhaps, each good poem is a kind of miracle birth, possessing a different ingenuity and metabolism. But poetry is a craft as well as an art, and the insights and techniques of craft, like carpentry, can be taught, learned, practiced, and relished.

For exercises corresponding to this chapter, please see page 155.

XII

FOR THE TEACHER AND USER

On the Use of Prompts, Exercises, and Skill-Building

A GOOD WRITING EXERCISE CAN RESULT IN A QUICKLY produced, often surprisingly successful poem. In that way, it offers an immediate gratification that can be useful in writing workshops and conferences. To a real student of poetry writing, however, the potential benefit of such exercises is much greater. Thoughtfully undertaken, a good exercise is a tutorial in craft, or a skill-building calisthenic, and it can enlarge your writing repertoire in permanent and profound ways.

When a person writes a certain kind of sentence (declarative, interruptive, interrogative), or when metaphor is employed in a particular way, or when the material of a poem is cast into long, end-stopped stanzas, a new neurological pathway is opened in the writer's brain. New linguistic possibilities—and abilities— are uncovered, new muscles are felt and flexed in the poetic anatomy. Potentially, each such discovery can enrich all the future poems undertaken by that writer.

It is not the abstract *theory* of a poetic exercise, or the juicy provocation of a premise, but the technical *enactment* that has a lasting, enriching effect on the talent of the apprentice. A new poetic strategy or gesture, completed, is stored in the muscle memory of the writer's poetic consciousness. To be analytically aware, of course, can only enhance the transformative effect of such exercises. Seen this way, every calisthenic exercise—even a seemingly rote one—is a rehearsal for the best poem you have ever written, which might spring into being next week or next month or ten years from now.

This handbook, *The Art of Voice*, could easily include twenty more chapters and a hundred more skill-building exercises. The topic of poetic voice, and the cleverness with which any distinct poet discovers and devises her or his own brand of voice, is an inexhaustible study—as mysterious and profound as the genetics of recombinant DNA.

What we hope is that these exercises will open doors for poets of all ages and encourage them to see poetic voice as a matter of artful exertion and craft, not accident or genius. The poet who can teach herself to search out and study the practices of technique in poetry has the potential to discover, improve, and evolve for a lifetime, and to enlarge the art of poetic possibility for all of us.

The Buddhists have a saying, "When the student is ready, the teacher will appear," but we don't believe in waiting around for the magic teacher. We believe in the adventure of work, and in diving deep and looking around. Maybe you could become your own best teacher. Implicitly, along those lines, we hope that these exercises suggest how you might formulate your own lessons from poems you discover and admire. Go forth, read widely, work hard, teach yourself. Then teach others.

EXERCISES

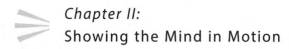

Chapter II:
Showing the Mind in Motion

Exercise 1: Gerald Stern's "Blue Skies, White Breasts, Green Trees"

Use the poem "Blue Skies, White Breasts, Green Trees" by Gerald Stern (from Chapter II) as a formal model for generating a speaker's poetic testimony of her mistakes, misunderstandings, and misperceptions.

> What I took to be a man in a white beard
> turned out to be a woman in a silk babushka
> weeping in the front seat of her car. . . .

Write the poem in a stanzaic form that resembles that of the model poem. Arrange the resulting material in a pattern that accentuates the diversity of examples—juxtaposing the extremely particular ("What I took to be a plastic bag with a goldfish in it") with something quite different ("turned out to be my former girlfriend with a gun in her hand").

Write a whole catalog of such units. In your next revision, sequence the poem's units in a way that progressively *escalates* the nature of the speaker's misunderstandings about the world. The poem should increase in intensity or enlarge in scale, as the speaker becomes more comic or more tragic, increasingly honest, or more personally real: "What I took to be true love / turned out to be an eight-dollar bottle of red wine / using me as a ventriloquist's dummy."

Exercise 2: Trying to Remember

Uncertainty may seem like an odd quality to cultivate in a poetic voice, but in fact our unsureness about what we think, see, feel, and remember is one of the most convincing dimensions of a human voice.

One of the ways of getting uncertainty on the page is through syntactical methods. Repetition, hesitation, self-revision, stutter, questions, self-interruption—these are a few of the devices for showing the speaker working through the effort of thinking.

In her poem "Old Wars," poet Caryl Pagel conjures up a speaker who wishes to tell a story but knows very few reliable facts of the tale; the poem, it turns out, is not about an old war but about the faltering voice of the speaker, about the sound of the uncertain remembering, of knowing, rather than information or theme:

You are trying to remember how
it happened   You are trying to
remember these events in a sensible

order   The narrator you think met
the old woman on a train
She had been to war or
at least you think you recall
reading that she said she had
The story started on the train
The narrator in this case was
mostly incidental. . . .

Use Pagel's poem as your model and write in the voice of a speaker trying to recall an event from the past or trying to figure something out about another person. In "Old Wars" Pagel uses the second-person (*you*) pronoun, but you should feel free to use the first-person singular (*I*) in your poem. Or you might use the third person (*he* or *they*). Perhaps your poem will discover a story line as it goes along, or perhaps not—in any case, experimenting with the voice of uncertainty is the goal of this exercise.

Here's an improvised example:

THE MYTH OF GREAT-GRANDMOTHER

We think her grave is in Cincinnati,
but it might be Pittsburgh with the rest of
her family, in a crowded cemetery. We think
she was a tall woman who didn't speak much,
or a lady of medium height who wouldn't stop talking.
She came in on a train and left on a train,
so goes the story, perhaps in the middle of the night.
She left a trail of dead husbands and happy babies

behind her, and she was wearing a black silk gown
when she made the remark we've been repeating
ever since, when the spring storms arrive:
"Here it comes," we say.
And we look around nervously, as if
she were coming back.

Exercise 3: The Mind in Motion— Thinking about Chance and Fate

Another model for showing the mind in motion is suggested
by Carl Dennis's poem "Two Lives," in which the speaker uses
imagination to envision the details of an alternative life he might
have led under different circumstances. Because such a framing hypothesis admits how much in our lives is sheer chance,
the poet's imagination is freed into a looseness that resembles
improvisation. The conceit is essentially playful, and the speaker's imagination roves into the past with a sense of wonder. Yet
Dennis's fantasy—for that is the mode of "Two Lives"—drifts
into larger, serious questions about the randomness of privilege
and the dubious justice of fate:

In my other life the B-17 my father is piloting
Is shot down over Normandy
And my mother raises her sons alone
On her widow's pension and on what she earns
As a nurse at the local hospital, . . .

. . . .

I play stickball after school in the lot
Behind the laundry. I come home bruised
From fistfights and snowball fights
With boys who live in the tenement on the corner.
Not once do I play with the boy I am
In this life, whose father, too old for the draft,
Starts a paint company in a rented basement

. . . .

In my other life, I have to leave high school
To bolster the family income as lab boy
In the building attached to the factory that in this life
My father owns. I clean test tubes and beakers,
With a break for stacking cans on the loading dock

. . . .

Serious reflection is only one option. Another poet might take the same hypothesis and handle it in a quite different tone, steering the poem toward a zanier, more kinetic kind of freedom. Here is an improvised example, mimicking the opening phrase from a David Lehman poem, "My name, if I were French. . . ." We can see where this could go—anywhere:

My name, if I were French, would be Lucien
and I would wear a beret and be a quiet master
at the art of flirtation. I would worship French women,
bow my head at high Mass, and later,

I would promenade the banks of the Seine,
and look with French eyes upon the French grass.

If I fished, the sleek fish I would catch
would be the poisson of France—
which would insist on being cooked
avec un splash of salt, fresh butter,
and served with a dry white Chardonnay
in a bottle of green glass as
dark and smoky as the Middle Ages in France.

Take this conceit, and the model of either the Dennis poem
"Two Lives" or the improvised version of the Lehman poem,
and write your own "What if" poem, "In my other life" poem,
or "My name, if I were French (German, Vietnamese, etc.)"
poem. Make your generation process an opportunity for invention on the level of images, narrative, and ideas about this "otherwise" life. The big themes hidden in this assignment for the
mind in motion are identity, desire, and character.

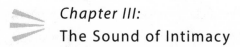

Chapter III:
The Sound of Intimacy

Exercise 1: Listen, Daisy . . .

Intimacy, you could say, is a matter of distance; for a writer, it
means to draw the reader *close*. One way to quickly create the
atmosphere of close proximity in a poem is to allow the reader
to "overhear" the speaker addressing a very familiar person in a
familiar way. Here is an example of such an address by the Portuguese poet Fernando Pessoa:

Listen, Daisy. When I die, although
You may not feel a thing, you must
Tell all my friends in London how much
My loss makes you suffer. Then go

To York, where you claim you were born
(But I don't believe a thing you claim),
To tell that poor boy who gave me
So many hours of joy (but of course

You don't know about that) that I'm dead.
Even he, whom I thought I sincerely
Loved, won't care . . . Then go and break

The news to that strange girl Cecily,
Who believed that one day I'd be great . . .
To hell with life and everyone in it!

(This form of making a specific intimate address to another person, by the way, has a rhetorical name, *apostrophe*.)

To properly admire this poem, notice how quickly and clearly the poet establishes the narrative context and motive for the speech. The speaker is addressing Daisy, giving her detailed instructions for how to act upon receiving the news of his demise—the situation is both comic and serious, and the tone is casual, yet also bossy, challenging, even a little sarcastic. In just a few lines, we learn a great deal about the speaker. Part of that effect of proximity may be created by the syntax of the first line, "Listen, Daisy. When I die, . . ." With this grammatical construction, we quickly are embedded in the middle of an intimate and forceful "plot"—an address that is also a story, dictated by a quirky speaker to a very specific other person. Though this monologue is not addressed to the "you" of the reader, the use of the second-person pronoun creates an intimate atmosphere. The reader feels she is given full access to the scene by the act of eavesdropping.

Write a poem beginning with an apostrophe to someone specific, giving them instructions on how to behave under certain circumstances. Be bossy but also self-revealing. Imitate the grammar which opens Pessoa's monologue, and you'll see how dynamic and effective it is.

For example:

"Look, Fred, when you get to Paris, try
not to embarrass yourself by asking
where the Eiffel Tower is. . . ."

Exercise 2: Speech Additives

Look at—and feel free to add to—the following list of "speech additives" below. Write a short monologue about some trivial subject or nonsubject, using a share of the samples listed here. If it helps, imagine a particular persona speaking—someone tough, or sentimental, for example.

Allow these additions of words and phrases to create a "voice" in your poem. Let the plot develop and throw in line breaks that enhance the rhythms of your speaker's voice and story. Then work the material, editing and moving parts around to achieve a more effective voice or poem.

well,	you see
hang on a sec	nobody knows
if you say so	you don't need a PhD to . . .
laugh if you like	why bother?
don't worry	anyway
don't you think?	and so forth
if you want to put it like that	fill in the blank for yourself
I'm the kind of person who . . .	sure enough
know what I mean?	for pete's sake
come to think of it	I mean
so I said	for better or for worse
who knows why	you tell me
like it or not	what am I supposed to
this isn't the first time	I have problems of my own
you see	and another thing
you can't tell me	know what I'm saying?
it's about time	been there, done that
see,	in fact
like I always say	you know what happened then
I couldn't believe it	such a shame, the old ladies sighed
I never saw it coming	There was nothing to say (but)

Here's an example:

THE FUTURE OF ITALIAN FOOD

We always make spaghetti with tomatoes—who knows
  why?
Laugh if you like, but if it's about color,
why not peppers for a change?
I've "questioned authority" before—don't ask,
you don't want to know—and you can't tell me
modern science can't find a new kind of
Italian cooking.
It's not brain surgery.
Linguine and pasta, it's Mama-food
originally made for grown-up babies in the Mafia.
That's a dangerous thing to monkey with,
but I'm the kind of person
who likes some change in the menu.
Life and death, they stay the same,
but you can't tell me Italian cuisine
isn't ready for a renovation,
know what I'm saying?

Exercise 3: Intimacy—Connecting through the Admission of Failure and Error

One limitation of many poems is that the speaker wants too much
to be liked and is consciously or unconsciously trying to make
a good impression on the reader—to convince others or themselves of their niceness, or their decency, or their wisdom. Par-

adoxically, however, such an agenda on the part of the speaker limits the development of intimacy with the reader.

In fact, one of the great services of poetry is to present a bravely unedited depiction of the human soul—full of anxieties, selfishness, guilt, and desire, as well as aspiration and hope. When a poem shows the less flattering aspects of a human consciousness and behavior, it releases the rest of us from our bondage to some imaginary level of perfection. The poetic voice that freely admits to failure, bewilderment, or error is a voice with which a reader can intimately identify. W. S. Merwin's poem "Fly" begins with such a blunt, un-self-flattering admission: "I have been cruel to a fat pigeon." The poem "Fate," by Sharon Olds, similarly commences, "Finally I just gave up and became my father." Such plain expression at the threshold of a poem establishes the reader and the speaker on the unpretentious ground we have in common: discouragement and self-awareness.

In this exercise, open the poem with an admission of failure or error: personal, professional, minor or major. Imagine a poem that begins, "My talk with Anne was a complete failure," or, "Turns out I believed too much in words," or, "Turns out I wasn't any good at French, / or wind surfing at the beach; Nor at biding my time in a relationship, / or waiting for the other person to discover that they loved me." Experiment with writing out of a voice (your own) that admits fault. Follow the poem where it goes after that, but the opening admission or confession of limitation can be a very effective way of drawing the reader into the circle of intimacy.

To generate some possibilities, you might consider asking these questions:

What stupid mistake can't your speaker forget?
What remembered mistake from the day before kept her
   awake last night?
What did your speaker forget to do this morning?
Why does your character secretly think they
   might be fired?
What mistake from his life does the speaker refuse to talk about?

(For another model, you can refer to Lisa Lewis's poem "While I'm Walking" in the text.)

Chapter IV:
The Warmth of Worldliness

The main way of enhancing your skill at the material imagination—at getting the world into your poems—is to make images, and to make a lot of them. Image making, and its cousin skill, metaphor making, is a muscle that develops with repetition and practice, like lifting barbells. Don't start with haiku, making one image at a time. Be excessive, be imperfect, and save your self-criticism for the revision process.

Exercise 1: Worldly Merchandise and Brand Names

This exercise is simple. Write a first-person narrative poem in which the brand name of a product appears in almost every line.

Let the narrative go where it will, but observe how the product naming lends a certain energy to the narrative.

> I was hanging out at the Food Court
> between WOK Heaven and Chicago Dogs,
> wearing my Sunday attire
> of purple Nikes and a Morrisey T-shirt,
> watching single moms in designer yoga pants
> breastfeed the future attorneys of Goldman Sachs. . . .

Exercise 2: Landscape and Weather

Read the opening of August Kleinzahler's poem "Snow in North Jersey," excerpted below, whose premise is simple (snow is falling) but whose images are clear, relaxed, and distinctive—the work of a writer who knows a particular landscape well. Identify and study what to you seem like the best images from his catalog. Then freely improvise a similar catalog of *things in weather*: scenes on which the rain or snow is falling or through which a cold wind is blowing. The "stem" of your litany should be simple and repetitive, the better to free your imagination for images: "Rain is falling on the doghouses of Houston; and on the used car lots, with their Jeep Cherokees and rusty Chevy Novas," and so on. Remember the law of *particularity*: the more concrete, the more clearly named, seen, or invented, the better the images will be. Again, write a lot of images, twenty or more, and notice how you gradually loosen up. Don't strive for big meanings but for vivid particularity. Let your ear, your imagination, and your memory all collaborate in the invention of images.

SNOW IN NORTH JERSEY

Snow is falling along the Boulevard
and its little cemeteries hugged by transmission shops
and on the stone bear in the park
and the WWI monument, making a crust
on the soldier with his chin strap and bayonet
It's blowing in from the west
over the low hills and meadowlands
swirling past the giant cracking stills
that flare all night along the Turnpike
. . . .
and the snow continues to fall and blanket
these crowded rows of frame and brick
with their heartbreaking porches and castellations
and the red '68 Impala on blocks
. . . .

Exercise 3: The Cascading Catalog of Images—Diane Seuss

Here is a third model to develop your image-making strengths: the Diane Seuss poem from Chapter IV, "Let's meet somewhere outside time and space." Using Seuss's opening, follow it with a ragtag catalog of images: simple ones, elaborate ones, sacred and profane ones, every kind. Note how Seuss uses parallel conjunctions to hold her images firmly in a grammatical sequence, and follow her example: "*Between* the Savings and Loan building and the recycling store," as she would say, "*Where* Daryll Bock meets Sarah Gompers on the sly after school." Write a page full of images like that. Loosen your image muscle. Draw from a broad spectrum of sources: vegetables, foreign countries, diseases, music. "Let's meet in Sweden, where Brahms is played to tuberculosis patients." Then, at some later time, go back and pick out the best moments in your writing. Revise the images, polish them, and arrange them in a sequence. Notice how they mysteriously improve, and how they contain narrative hints to the inner personality of your own imagistic depths and history.

Chapter V:
The Tribal Bond of the Vernacular

As native speakers of English and experts on American culture, we are much more polylingual, really, than we give ourselves credit for. We may not speak Italian, or Serbian, or French, but we're keenly attuned to the speech styles of other people, and we're skilled at ventriloquism and mimicry. We have an idea of how millionaires and surfers, policemen and telemarketers talk.

In John Weir's prose poem "The Beautiful American Word 'Guy,' " the speaker considers all the different ways that men address each other casually, and how each form of address carries its own complex social connotations. In the course of his meditation, he conjures up many small scenarios and speakers to exemplify these male interactions—insulting, friendly, passionate, snide, ironic, sincere. Weir's poem is a guided tour of the vernaculars of masculinity:

The beautiful American word "guy." It always gets me. For one thing, a guy is never alone. What if your name were Guy? Then you'd think that all the men behind all the deli counters on Ninth Avenue were talking to you. "What'll it be, Guy?" "Mayo, Guy?" "We're outta sesame, Guy, how about onion?" Guy is friendly, whereas "man" is hostile and competitive. "I hear you, man," actually means, "Back off, dickhead, I'm in charge here." "Dude" is useful, but thanks to Bart Simpson it's never sincere. "Buddy," "buster" and "pal" are sturdy but tainted by camp, like dialogue from old Hollywood movies. "Boss" scares me, and "chief" sounds undemocratic and maybe politically incorrect.

I like "brother" sometimes. "Brother, you gotta be kidding," a truck driver yelled at me once on Eighth Avenue, because I was reading a book and crossing the street against the light. He twisted the word around to mean, "Die, motherfucker," but I'm a romantic, and I heard him saying, "Cling to me as we plunge together manfully into the abyss."

Still, guy is the most inclusive and universally tender, taking the back of your neck in its creased palm and saying, "I'm counting on you." It's a promise and a threat, a stroke, a supplication, and a plea. If there were an epic poem of America in muscular four-beat Old English lines, its first word would not be "Hwaet," but "Guy."

Exercise 1: The Beautiful
American Word _____

Using Weir's poem as a model, think of an American word or phrase that has a particular vernacular meaning and circumstances—it might be "honey," or "sugar," or "slam dunk," or "chill," or "hookup," or "presidential," "tight-ass," "loser," "sissy," "weirdo," "dude," "stuck up," "princess," "bummer," "special," "breakup," "out to lunch," "party," "brouhaha."

Once you have chosen a word or phrase, explore the alternative synonyms and vernacular expressions that might be employed for the same occasion in different social settings. Invent vignettes about who would be using it, when speaking to whom, and under what circumstances. Consider your poem a kind of personal essay or lecture about this "beautiful American" expression. Have fun, but also don't be afraid to be serious in your exploration of the temperament and the linguistic layers of American social realities.

Exercise 2: Suddenly There Is . . .

It does not take all that much vernacular speech to trigger the warm sense of recognition a reader requires to feel comfortable; our ears are keenly tuned to the "native" element of our verbal idiosyncrasy. Grace Paley's poem "Suddenly There's Poughkeepsie" makes that simple claim to naturalness from its very beginning, with her word choices and tone tuned to a plain folksy style:

what a hard time
the Hudson River has had
trying to get to the sea

it seemed easy enough to
rise out of Tear of
the Cloud and tumble
and run in little skips
and jumps   draining
            a swamp here and
    there   acquiring
streams and other smaller
rivers with similar
longings for the wide
imagined water

suddenly
there's Poughkeepsie
except for its spelling
an ordinary town but
the great heaving
ocean sixty miles away. . . .

The opening conceit, or idea, of Paley's poem—to sympathize with the big river—is charmingly fresh, but it is the familiar vernacular clothing of the speaker's voice that makes us feel that we are listening from home, comfortably seated in a favorite rocking chair. "What a hard time," she says, "the Hudson River has had." . . . She says, "it seemed easy enough," and goes on from there, improvising and sympathizing with a force of nature. Paley's speaker sticks to the facts, ecological and geological, about the Hudson River, but her vernacular manner positions her in relation to both the river and the reader. Once again, it is remarkable to note what an essential influence "inessential" words and phrases have in a poem.

For your exercise, follow Paley's model and express sympathy, or blame, or judgment toward some force or phenomenon of nature: a season, the element of fire, the mouse in the attic, the color blue, etc. Emulate Paley's short line breaks if you like and notice how that visual presentation affects the pace of the poem. Try to find phrases drawn from common culture to sustain the relaxed and populist tone of Paley's poem.

Exercise 3: Tribal Lingo

Think of a profession, a trade, a tribe, a social class, or a gang that has its own inside lingo and technical vocabulary, its own vernacular: short-order cooks, long-distance truckers, hip-hop artists, divorce lawyers, pre-med students, junkies, police officers, yoga teachers, psychiatrists, carpenters, auto mechanics.

Select one of these cultural "tribes" and brainstorm a generous list of likely vocabulary and phrases for that demographic group. Then write a poem in that voice using that vernacular. Observe how subject matter and style collaborate in the generative process. Don't be cautious about exaggerating attitudes and narrative circumstances; anything that loosens your imagination is good for the poem and can be trimmed back later if necessary.

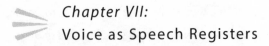

Chapter VII:
Voice as Speech Registers

Exercise 1: The Thing About Julius Caesar Is That He Really Liked to Boogie

As the chapter on speech registers makes clear, to move between high, middle, and low tones in a poem is one of the most effective ways for the personality of the speaker to display itself through voice. What does it mean to shift registers in a poem? Recall, from Chapter V, the first lines of Marie Howe's poem "Reading Ovid":

> The thing about those Greeks and Romans is that
>   at least mythologically,
>
> they could get mad. . . .

When Howe takes on the subject of Roman gods, the first poetic choice she makes is to lower the tone of the discourse through her use of vernacular speech registers: "the thing about . . ." she says, "they could get mad." In a sense she is "translating" the classical stories into contemporary diction and a more intimate mode, thus reassuring the reader that this allegedly "high culture" tells stories that we regular middle-brow mortals can relate to.

As with any skill, the best way to get a handle on speech registers is to learn by *doing* rather than by thinking. Howe's stylistic experiment is easy enough to use as the launching pad for your own poem. Consider, for example, a poem that might open,

"The thing about Julius Caesar is that he really liked to boogie."
Or, "The thing about those Jane Austen girls, they partied like
Beyoncé." Thus your poem from the start creates a speaker who
is explaining a "high-register" subject matter in low or middle
register. Take a highbrow subject and treat it in a lowbrow manner and see where it takes you.

Exercise 2: Low Subject, High Style

This poetic experiment with the tone of a speaker's voice also works
in the reverse direction: not by treating high subject matter in a low
register, but by elevating the low into a high mode. It is invigorating
to take a subject usually thought too humble for poetry and treat it
with the verbal style of high poetry. "Ode to My Hamburger," for
example, has potential; ditto "Ode to My Asthma Inhaler," "Ode to
My Father's Silence," "Ode to the Disposable Diaper."

Here's what such an exercise in stretching the conventions of
speech register looks like in the hands of the adroit poet Bar-
bara Hamby:

ODE TO MY 1977 TOYOTA

Engine like a Singer sewing machine, where have you
    not carried me—to dance class, grocery shopping,
into the heart of darkness and back again? O the fruit
    you've transported—cherries, peaches, blueberries,
watermelons, thousands of Fuji apples—books,
    and all my dark thoughts, the giddy ones, too,

like bottles of champagne popped at the wedding of two
   people
      who will pass each other on the street as strangers
in twenty years. Ronald Reagan was president when I
   walked
      into Big Chief Motors and saw you glimmering
on the lot like a slice of broiled mahi mahi or sushi
      without its topknot of tuna. Remember the months
I drove you to work singing "Some Enchanted Evening"?
      Those were scary times. All I thought about
was getting on I-10 with you and not stopping. . . .

If you are in doubt about what high-register English poetry
sounds like, glance at the language and syntax of one of the great
odes of Romantic poetry such as John Keats's "To Sleep":

O soft embalmer of the still midnight,
   Shutting, with careful fingers and benign,
Our gloom-pleas'd eyes, embower'd from the light,
   Enshaded in forgetfulness divine:
O soothest Sleep! if so it please thee, close
   In midst of this thine hymn my willing eyes,
Or wait the "Amen," ere thy poppy throws
   Around my bed its lulling charities.

Then, like Hamby, ventriloquize Keats's high-register language
onto your chosen (humble) topic, allowing the language and the
syntax of the poem to elevate it.

Exercise 3: Using Contradiction Between Speech Register and Social Occasion

Another way to play with, and thus to learn about, the manipulation of poetic registers is to write a poem whose *stated* intent is different from its *true* intent. Thus, to write a poem of apology for something for which the speaker is in fact *not* sorry creates a tonal tension that is intriguing and revealing. Similarly, to write a thank-you poem for something that one would not feel gratitude about is an effective premise for a poem because it has immediate tonal "torque."

As an illustration, consider "Thank You" by the poet John Skoyles, in which the speaker offers somewhat ironic thanks to an ex-girlfriend:

Thank you for leaving me
talking to myself in your voice,
and thank you for everything I said
about your needing me.

And for my invention of so many pet names,
thank you. They could have been heard
only by someone in love, in bed.

And thank you for making me so aware
of the pain of something said,
and the pain of something not said.

And for stopping me from thinking
what might have been, thanks,
because when you think like that

you're already in the past tense
and someone's got to bring you out of it,
thank you.

Following Skoyles's example, write a poem in which the speaker expresses gratitude for some misfortune or mistreatment at the hands of the universe: "Thank You for Taking My Parking Space," "Thank you for Stealing My Computer, Thief," etc.

Exercise 4: Speech Registers

The reverse experiment has equal poetic potential: not an insincere *thank you* but an insincere *I'm sorry*. To apologize for eating the last of the dessert in the refrigerator (when you are not at all sorry), or to apologize for missing an event that you didn't want to attend, has the charming ring of ironic truth. Such a tonal stance is strong because it frames a well-known social reality: the discrepancy between what good manners require and our real feelings. That is solid ground for poetry to stand on. James Laughlin's "It Does Me Good," whose title serves as the first line of the poem, performs this kind of tonal double entendre, creating complexity by seeming to praise the practice of self-humiliation:

to bow my body to the ground
when the emperor passes I am

one of the gardeners at the
palace but I have never seen

his face when he walks in the
garden he is preceded by boys

who ring little bells and I
bow myself down when I hear

the bells. . . .

Laughlin's use of situational tone makes his apparently simple poem provocative as well as charming. The servant says, "It does me good," but, we wonder, is he really grateful for his obligation to prostrate himself? We can't really tell, but the possibility that he is speaking with some hint of irony is provocative. Poems can be ambiguous, entertaining, and surprisingly true all at the same time. Here, your exercise is to take the strategy of one of these poems and write a poem that creates a flavorful contradiction between the speech register and the occasion. Write an apology-you-don't-mean poem.

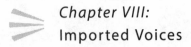

Chapter VIII:
Imported Voices

We commonly think of poems as the literary genre most *intended* for individual sincerity and perhaps most perfectly designed for the solitary voice. That is why lyric poems are often described as dramatic *monologues*—speeches delivered by a single passionate and earnest speaker.

Thank goodness this is not the whole truth. In fact, there are an infinite number of ways to enrich the contents of your poem with secondary voices, turning the poem into a more social environment: a conversation, an argument, a salon. Take a look at the opening of Matthew Siegel's quiet and delightful poem "By the Flowers at the Supermarket":

At the supermarket the floral woman asks me
if I need any help. *Complicated question*, I reply

and spend a few minutes dipping my face
into the rising breath of the flowers.

I'm ready to be helped now, I tell her
and she asks what my intentions are.

I'd like the girl to see that I can have flowers
inside a big glass jar on my coffee table just to look at

and I don't need them to be beautiful,
just a little scent in case she does not return.

When another character in Seigel's narrative asks the primary speaker, do you need any help, and he is given the opportunity to say, "*Complicated question*," we are in a rich echo chamber of implication, metaphor, and resonance. We understand that the speaker is anxious and may indeed need help—perhaps more help than can be found in a florist's shop. A moment later, when the speaker is asked what his "intentions" are, we are attuned to the complex social inferences of that word, *intentions*, in the context of romance. Seigel's use of a secondary speaker, the clerk at the florist's shop, imports a host of complex social inferences into the poem. We sense that a real conversation is taking place, even if mostly in the insecure interior voice of the narrator, and we sense that this moment has both a background and a future.

Imagine Seigel's poem as a single-person monologue, and you can discern that it would probably be less energetically complex, less nuanced, and less poignant. As so often occurs in poems that include secondary speakers, "By the Flowers at the Supermarket" has the quality of a game of ping-pong, of an unpredictable and revealing back-and-forthness. Without the interactive *friction* between the two speech agendas of these speakers, the poem would carry less feeling, less mystery, and less meaning.

Exercise 1: Using Multiple Speakers— Naming and Renaming

We sometimes forget that in a poem, the poet can have anyone say anything in any manner. In fact, a poem can contain a dozen or a hundred different speakers, each one saying something different in a different style. Such a poem still needs to be bound together by, perhaps, commonality of subject. Consider the subject of death, for example, and how many distinct stylistic ways there are to report the death of another person:

I regret to inform you that Mr. Seale is deceased.
Bob was dead.
The patient's vital functions declined at nine thirty.
Cardiac and respiration became undetectable.
Time of expiration was recorded at 9:42.
Death, our ancient enemy, had delivered its bouquet.
Now the cliffs of memory begin to crumble.
What's his name had definitely kicked the bucket.

Write a poem in which multiple speakers are weighing in on the same topic. The speakers may be humble or famous; they may speak in elaborate syntax and vocabulary or crudely. The principal linguistic activity is naming and renaming. Let yourself use exaggerated metaphors, slang, euphemisms, whatever, for referring to the object of discussion. Here's a quickly improvised poem that uses multiple speakers to explore the broad range of perspectives one might have on a common modern appliance:

BOOB TUBE

Jillian says that television is the great blue bosom
through which Americans like to suck forgetfulness.

Joey says that if you have HBO, the moon
comes to seem over-rated.

Emily Dickinson never wrote a poem that begins, *Because
    I did not stop for death,*
I turned to CNN.

Robert says that TV is a true friend to the sick and the
    afflicted.

But Dorothy Parker said *If I can't eat it, drink it or sleep with it,*
what good is it?

Travis says television can't compete with beer
and Phil says the Iroquois call it the last hope of Native
    People,

a remark which nobody understands;
and which the Iroquois, those mysterious people,

refuse to explain.

Exercise 2: Writing a Poem by Challenging Poetic Speech

Poems often succeed by overturning the reader's expectations
of what a poem is, of what poetry itself is, and of what a poem

sounds like. A great anthology could be made by collecting such antipoetic poems, poems that gain some of their energy by attacking the conventional conception of poetry: the expectation of "pretty" images, sweet sentiments, florid linguistic lushness, or simpering delicacy. In "A Little Poem About the Rain," John Engman launches his poem by offering a sample of "how a poem *should* start":

> *There is a chance of rain on Minnehaha Avenue.*
> That's how a poem should start. But they won't pay
> for little poems about the rain—they want "art."
> Why didn't you take notes at the poetry workshop?

"There is a chance of rain on Minnehaha Avenue," says the poet—his quotation marks are implied, and his initial example is followed by commentary, then other examples of how a poem is forbidden to start.

> Don't say you drove the lonely avenues of rain.
> Don't say rain whispered harsh words to the moon.
> Don't say someone you love has left you nothing
> to say but the moon on lonely avenues of rain.

Write a poem in which you borrow the rhetoric of Engman's beginning and substitute your own version of what the language of a poem "should" sound like. In its first two lines, it sets up two kinds of speech—"poetic" and "nonpoetic"—in contrast to each other. In your poem, you might want to invent an exaggerated version of poetic speech to start with, like "My heart is a trembling spiderweb in rain," or "Ye Gods! Forsake not my forlorn soul. / That's how a poem should start." Then see what develops as you shuttle back and forth between your two styles of voice.

Chapter IX:
Voices Borrowed from the Environment

The world is full of literary forms waiting to be hijacked and turned into vehicles for poems. Police reports, announcements through airport intercoms, lost-and-found notices, recipes—all of these are shared verbal conventions and formulas, with their own style and tone, that can be adapted to more personal or soulful ends.

Exercise 1: Reviews

Write a book (restaurant, food) review of one of your ex-boyfriends or -girlfriends. Or write the book review that one of your exes would write about you, to let prospective customers know what they have to look forward to. As research, read reviews on YELP or other websites and notice the tone, the style, and some of the terminology of those evaluative genres.

Here's a book-review example:

SLAVE OLD MAN

Patrick Chamoiseau, trans. from the French and Creole by Linda Coverdale (New Press)

Somewhere between a fever dream and a prose poem, Chamoiseau's short novel is about a slave who escapes a plantation in Martinique, pursued by a mythical mastiff. As the old man enters the forest and mystically encounters Martinique's past, the astounding sensorial prose develops an almost tangible rhythm: "He stocks his soul with scattered, reconstructed, lopsided things, which weave him a shimmering memory. Often, at night, this memory crushes him with insomnia." This novel is a transfixing, profound experience.—Gabe Habash, deputy reviews editor, *Publishers Weekly*

Somewhere between a fever dream
and a dietician, my ex-boyfriend Jason
is a tall man with a short attention span.
Perfect summer reading he may seem,
but be forewarned that the action-packed first chapter
flattens into a long middle narrative
of watching cable TV and dates canceled
at the last moment. That irresistible look
of a lost puppy is one of Jason's greatest assets—you'll love
    it at first.
Then Jason becomes something of a dog without a leash,
who doesn't call or let you know

where the relationship is going. You turn the page
   expectantly
and one day, he never comes back. Good luck.

Exercise 2: Police Reports

Take the language of the improvised police report below and change the details to accommodate stories from minor domestic "offenses," like leaving the milk on the countertop or failing to wash the dishes on Thursday night after dinner. Likewise, for Exercise 3, borrow the language of the airport intercom announcement to structure a poem.

BURGLARY, MORRIS PLACE:

At approximately 11:10 PM on 9/12/18 police received a call regarding a home burglary. The reporting party told police he returned home to find his $300 portable beer machine missing. The victim suspected his girlfriend's ex-boyfriend of the theft. Prior to placing a call to police, the victim drove by the ex-boyfriend's house where he thought he saw his portable beer machine under a blanket on the seat of the suspect's vehicle. Police confronted the suspect, who denied the accusations. Later the stolen property was found in the suspect's garage. The victim declined to press charges.

Exercise 3: The Airport Intercom Announcement

Paging passenger Woolf, Virginia Woolf,
incoming on American Airlines Flight 1302 from
  Cleveland.
Please meet your party at the chicken curry concession
  near Concourse C,
and try to keep an open mind.
He will be wearing an Emily Dickinson baseball cap
and a necklace of red flowers
and he has nothing to apologize for.
You'll see him in front of the magazine stand,
where they do not carry the *New York Times*; please do
try to keep that impatient expression off your face.
The next part of your life is going to be more fun than you
  think.

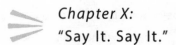

Chapter X:
"Say It. Say It."

Exercise 1: Big Assertions

With practice, one can cultivate and refine one's facility with
assertion and abstraction—they are, in their way, as inventive
and particular as images. Just as descriptive or narrative skills
develop through study and practice, the same is true of abstract
declaration.

Here are some examples of forceful, somewhat creative assertions:

Sometimes it is right to tell a lie.
Every family is a kind of prison.
Part of being everything is mud.
Each one has their hidden wound.
Love is not a fatal disease.
A surprise is an ugly experience.
Every poem is a description of heaven or hell.

Here is the exercise: teach yourself to be unafraid of big assertions. Think of yourself as a maker of hypothetical truths, brazenly making up wise or slightly outrageous sayings about life. Write a 12–13 (approx) -line poem in which you employ and deploy one of these statements, or a statement with a similar kind of authority and rhythm. Your assertion should be compact and memorable. The poem should be narrative and tell a short story. Try placing your statement in various positions in the poem and observe which position is the most interesting or effective.

Exercise 2: "Emotion Is an Exacting Science"

Write a ten-line poem in which the closing single authoritative statement is "Emotion is an exacting science." That sentence is the only abstract statement allowed in the poem. All other lines and sentences must be narrative or descriptive, probably including characters and scenes. For example: "Lilly walked the dog."

"The telephone rang but no one picked it up." "In Malaysia whole families sleep together when the monsoon comes." "Emotion is an exacting science." Be concrete and particular. Now arrange and revise the poem in such a way that the statement positioned in the poem's last line connects with the details in revealing and resonant ways.

Exercise 3: Analyzing Structural Arrangement

Go through a well-made meditative-narrative poem with a pen or highlighter and circle or identify the distinct elements: abstract assertions, images, narrative, metaphors. Figure out the architectural structure of the poem and how it is staged; where does it shift in tone or transition between two stories, or in voice, or in register? Which are the most important moments in the poem? Intellectually? Emotionally? How is the development of the poem *paced*? What sections or constituent stages could it be broken into? Is there any place where the poem drags, takes too long or not long enough?

Try typing out the text of the poem line by line; invent your own system of terminology for what the types of ingredients are and how they fit together. Some recommended poems for such analysis might be Philip Larkin's "This Be the Verse," Jane Hirschfield's "Tree," Jane Kenyon's "Man Eating," Marianne Moore's "A Grave."

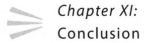

Chapter XI:
Conclusion

As the preceding chapters on voice often emphasize, an individual self is more diverse than we commonly acknowledge. Whether we are describing an autobiographical self or an other, it is the multiplicity of the psyche and the contradictions in human nature that make the most interesting portraits, whether of self or other.

The great twentieth-century pioneers of psychology—Freud, Jung, and others—shocked their generation by asserting that the beast and the angel, the male and the female, the child and the parent are simultaneous citizens of the republic of the self. Our inconsistencies of behavior, feeling, and thought are evidence of our internal particularity and our rich complexity. Each of us is a crowd of voices, alternately squabbling and reconciling.

A good poem that takes the self as its subject must always be on guard against oversimplification of the self, against sentimental idealizations or simplistic vilifications. Fortunately, there are many innovative poetic methods for representing the multiplicity of the self.

In her poem "My Mother Says," Kimberly Bruss practices a radical poetic strategy: to completely forgo the convention of a poetic moderator and editorial commentary and to arrange many different *kinds* of detail in counterpoint as a method of portraiture. The point Bruss makes with her experiment is how diverse a human being can be—reverent, profane, sarcastic, witty, bossy, insightful, protective, selfish, vain, angry, etc. As you read her poem, consider how many different tones, textures, anecdotes, and exclamations coexist inside what turns out to be a compassionate and interesting portrait of the speaker's mother:

Your father drinks weak coffee.

Vacuum the dead moths from behind the window screen.
Their powdered wings look like ghosts against the glass
    and you know how I'm superstitious.

I talked with the cat this morning.
She's upset with you.
She said you'd know why.

My morning got away from me.

We live in a fucking zoo.

I couldn't stand your father at first.
He drove a motorbike and had long, brown hair.
And he never read anything longer than a magazine article
    or a menu page.
But he took me to the airport on our first date.
We parked in a field and lay on the hood of his car,
    watching the planes take off and land.

Kelly, Kristen, Kimberly, Kimberly, Kimberly.

When I go to church, I want to feel something moving
   above me.

The garden smells like tomatoes ripening.
Your father gave me a tomato on our second date that I ate
   over the sink while he watched.

Whore.
I love the way that word feels in my mouth.
Whore, whore.

Try to keep up with me.

I kind of have a knack for these things.

I used to tell the dog to play in traffic.
But then I stopped, because I knew it would be my fault if
   he actually did.

Who put a wet towel down the laundry chute?
I will have your head.

I woke at dawn to feed the birds.
Have you seen them all?
I sat with a book and pretended to read and sometimes
   there are so many of them, I have trouble breathing.

This morning chickadees and swallows swarmed me.
The closest I've been to flying.

Where is my boy? Oh where, where is my boy?

Exercise 1: My Mother Says

Your exercise is to borrow Bruss's title—which, you will notice, packages the poem with a narrative frame that is both economical and broadly capacious: "My Mother Says." First, generate a wide range of remarks made by your poetic subject. Do not limit yourself to an obvious idea of character consistency; there is no room for sentimentality or easy vilification in this "portrait." Include both flattering and unflattering details, errantly quirky tones, and skewed samples of self. In preparation, you might even go through Bruss's poem and identify, if you can, the type and tone of each installment in her portrait.

Once your motley materials have come to hand, the poetic challenge is in the arrangement, or orchestration, of the units in sequence and music.

Exercise 2: Things My Father Never Said

Now choose a figure who is not too emotionally close to you for you to write about *inventively*. Instead, choose someone at a greater distance from your own life—Christopher Columbus in 1492, or the president, or your distant uncle who lives in Canada.

Or you might choose to *reverse* the assignment, in a poem called, for example, "Things My Father Never Said," a catalog of things the speaker's father may have hypothetically thought but did not voice, or remarks that he would never have spoken out loud, like these improvised samples:

I don't care about the Dow Jones report for Tuesday, June 19, 2018.
As long as the kids don't block my view of the television.
Nobody really likes classical music.
I'd like to steal Kevin Young's Camaro and put it in a ditch for him.
I'm Irish—I already knew the pope is full of shit.
To have children is the most terrifying thing in the world.
Sometimes you just want them to screw up and get it over with.
That Grand Funk Railroad concert in the seventies—
don't tell anyone, but it changed my life.
Even a blind hog finds an acorn now and then.
I don't remember much about my mother,
but I remember the feel of rain on my face at work this morning.
It's amazing how much people think about, how much they *suffer*, over
what to eat for dessert.
Funny, isn't it, how nuclear war isn't scary anymore?

The polar bear is a very photogenic animal; we should get
more of them.

That's what you want, is it? Me sharing more of my
feelings?

Better be careful what you wish for.

I'm going to fix the back fence now like I said I would.

That retaining wall makes me feel like a man—an old one,
but a man.

COMPLETE LIST OF POEMS REFERENCED

Mentioned:

ACKNOWLEDGMENTS

Quite a few friends read drafts of this book and provided valuable feedback: warm thanks to each of them. Thank you to Jill Bialosky and her team at W. W. Norton. Thank you to Melissa Flamson and her permissions crew.

CREDITS